Homemaking for Happiness

Books by Mrs. White

Mother's Faith

For the Love of Christian Homemaking

Early Morning Revival Challenge

Mother's Book of Home Economics

Living on His Income

Old Fashioned Motherhood

Economy for the Christian Home

Mother's Hour

At Mother's House

Introduction to Home Economics

An Old Fashioned Budget

Homemaking for Happiness

{Cover Photo: Parlour table, at Mrs. White's home.}

Homemaking for Happiness

Wonderful Days at Home

The Legacy of Home Press
puritanlight@gmail.com

Homemaking for Happiness
Copyright 2021 by Mrs. Sharon White
All Rights Reserved.

The content of this book has been gathered from previously published posts from "The Legacy of Home" blog, and "Letters from the Estate," private newsletters, written by Mrs. Sharon White. These were originally published during the years of 2018 to 2021.

No portion of this book may be copied without permission from the publisher.

The Legacy of Home Press
ISBN: 978-0-578-91863-1

Homemaking for Happiness: Wonderful Days at Home
Author – Mrs. Sharon White

Contents

Introduction	11
Spring	13
1. I Don't Want to Miss Dinner	15
2. Standard of Living	17
3. Don't Forget the Cheetos, Me`me	21
4. Spring Housekeeping in Winter	23
5. A Surprise Supper	26
6. The Little Jobs of Spring Cleaning	29
7. Easter Morning	31
8. A Comforting Sick Room	33
9. Neglecting the Housework	37
10. The Secret to a Happy Home	40
11. Checking on the Gardens	46
12. Difficult Times with the Family	48
13. Housekeeping with an Injury	52
14. Restraining Domestic Spending	54
15. The Full Pantry	56
16. What Did You Do Today?	59
17. Patience and Faith While Staying Home	61
18. Make an Effort	65
19. Help for Staying Home During the Crisis	67

20. I Don't Want to Miss a Blessing	70
21. Confined to the Second Floor	72
22. Reviving the Prayer Journal	74
23. Flowers for the Dinner Table	77
24. Missing the Lilacs	80
25. Church in the Living Room	82
26. Waiting for the Door to be Opened	84
27. Old Time Store Clerks	86
28. Bible School at Home	89
29. Peace Be Upon This House	92

Summer — 97

30. Please Use Real Dishes	99
31. Travel Budget	101
32. Comfort from the Hymn Book	103
33. The Slacker and the Messy House	105
34. Simple Days at Home	107
35. Financial Peace for 25 cents	110
36. A Day of Homemaking	112
37. Writing Letters by the Lantern	114
38. Summer Heat in Rural Vermont	116
39. The Anniversary of a Family	118
40. The Four Little Tasks of Home	121
41. Evening Devotions	124
42. One Must Not Complain	126
43. Passing the Time in the Kitchen	128

44. Don't Forget the Bell	130
45. Keeping a Frugal Kitchen	131
46. Paper Napkins for Grand-girl	134
47. Heritage of Family Bibles	136
48. Supplies for the Household	139
49. An Evening Walk in the Garden	141
50. Poor in Spirit	143
51. Little Walks in the Garden	145
52. Enough Money to be Content	147
53. Old Time Homemaking	149

Autumn — 153

54. Days of Housekeeping	155
55. Sewing in the Guest Room	159
56. At Grandmother's House	161
57. Domestic Happiness	164
58. I Want to Be A Mama	168
59. A New England Winter on a Small Income	170
60. Old Fashioned Revival Hour	175
61. In the Quiet of the Morning	177
62. Chores for Grandchildren	179
63. Two Days Off	181
64. A Sweet Little Visitor	183
65. Pacing Oneself to Keep House	186
66. The Day I Quit Gardening	189
67. Peaceful Homemaking	192

68. Treats from the Kitchen	195
69. Getting a Fire in the Morning	197
70. School Work for Grandmother	199
71. Keep Traditions Alive	201
72. The Organized Home	204
73. The Boarding School	206
74. Chasing Butterflies	211
75. Every Day is a Gift	214
76. Keep Rebuilding the Home	216
77. Finding Warmth by the Fire	220
78. Cheering Up the Home	223
79. A Humble Thanksgiving	226
80. Walking with a Hymn Book	229
81. Lemon for your Tea	231
Winter	233
82. Christmas Snow Storm in Vermont	235
83. Mother's Homemade Birthday Tea	237
84. An Evening Out	241
85. The Homemaking List	244
86. Confined to Home	247
87. Slow and Steady Homemaking	250
88. Well Rested	252
89. Mottoes in a Humble Home	255
90. Church Clothes	259
91. Diary of a Clean House	260

92. Proper Speaking	268
93. The Benefit of Staying Home	271
94. Playing the Food Game	274
95. The Day I Did Not Meet Franklin Graham	275
96. Focus on the Home	277
97. Christmas Tea Party	280
98. Strength to do What is Right	283
99. Detached from Technology	285
100.- Reading Through the Bible with Mister	286
101.- The Noon Meal	290
102.- Go on Sowing	292
103.- Keeper of the House	294
104.- Clothing Allowance	297
105.- Waiting Out the Cold Winter Months in Vermont	300
106.- A Christmas Break	303

Introduction

In this book, you will find essays, articles, and diary entries about life in a Christian home. I have been a housewife for more than 30 years. My husband ("Mister," or "Papa," as the grandchildren call him) and I have 5 grown children and 12 grandchildren.

Entries are like visits to our home, and are arranged by season. These include: "Keeping a Frugal Kitchen;" "Missing the Lilacs;" "An Evening Walk in the Garden;" "At Grandmother's House;" and "Chores for Grandchildren."

You will also find photographs showing a little of the local landscape.

You will notice some of the entries have dates from the year 2020. There are times when a crisis in the world (in the culture or economy) will affect life at home. We will all encounter difficult times, in our families, and in life – in - general. Through it all, we must do our best to cheer each other along and to stay strong. We can try to bear things sweetly, ministering to others, helping in any way we can. I once heard my Mother describe a terrible ordeal a relative had gone through. My Mother praised this dear lady, by saying, "She behaved herself beautifully." I will never forget that.

I hope you will find encouragement in these pages.

Spring

{Photograph on Previous Page: The back grounds of Mrs. White's property.}

1

I Don't Want to Miss Dinner

I had such a busy day with the family. We had a few errands and then company came to visit. This was some of my children and grandchildren. There was cleaning and baking and cooking to do. But I was also recovering from an illness, so I was more worn out than ever. Regardless, I will always enjoy the family and the work, to the best of my ability.

For some reason, by late afternoon, I was so tired I wanted to fall asleep. The house was quiet. The company had gone home. I was sitting in the living room with Papa (my husband). I wanted to know what he would like for dinner. He just smiled at me. He knew how very tired we both were. He didn't think I should bother. "Don't worry about it. I will just make myself something later."

I told him I would make Fettuccini Alfredo for him and that I would have pumpernickel toast and tea. We would each have our own meal, but sit together at the table. It would be just simple food. We needed to eat anyway, so why not have a little precious time together for the evening meal. I could have easily taken my toast on a tray and rested in bed. He would have been happy in front of the television with his plate. Yes, we could easily do our own thing with whatever food we came up with. But I needed something more than just rest. I needed the beautiful time of sitting together at the table. I told him, sadly, "I don't want to miss dinner."

After spending the day being so busy and active, I didn't want to miss the experience of sitting at the table with him and eating a quiet meal. I wanted to use a tablecloth and set the table. I wanted salt and pepper shakers in the middle, even if we did not use them. I wanted the experience of dinner. I didn't want to miss sitting with my husband and hearing him say a prayer before the meal.

We had such a quiet, happy time at the kitchen table. He said a prayer of thanks for the food. I love to hear Papa's prayers. He enjoyed the Fettuccini and even had a second helping. I ate my toast slowly so we could visit as we ate. The dinner hour is such a blessed time to be together with the family and enjoy nourishing food. No matter how tired I get, I love the experience of the evening meal. This is what helps bond the family.

2
Standard of Living

In a 1970's sermon by Billy Graham, he talked about the way he lived as a child. His family lived on a large farm in the country. There was no running water. There was no electricity. They had no radio or television. I believe he said they did not even have a car. But they had food and warmth and were loved at home. He talked about how nearly every family lived the same way. He mentioned that our current standard of living was getting much higher.

My own father lived on a farm. His family were sharecroppers in the rural south. They had a simple home that his mother took care of. Each day, she would pray with her husband and help him get up, early each morning, so he could go to work. He held down a regular job, helped the family with the farming, and was a revival preacher. His time was focused on eternal matters, practical survival, and the love and care of his family. They did family altar each evening before bed. They went to church every single time the doors were open. It was a traditional old- time family life, much like the home where Billy Graham grew up in. This was a common type of life, at one point, in our nation's history.

In the Massachusetts neighborhood where I grew up, we had cozy homes in our suburban town. Many of them were cottages that were built by our grandfathers. We lived old time, traditional lives. We were thrifty, careful in our saving and spending, and did not require much. Now, all these years later, the wealthy crowd has come in and is buying up all the old cottages. These are mainly two-income couples, with careers in the city of Boston. They want to commute out to the beautiful suburban town. They are tearing down our grandfather's cottages and building (literally) million-dollar houses in their place. It raises the standard of living, the property taxes for all, and makes it impossible for common families to afford to purchase a home. I am grateful we moved, some years ago, out in the country of Vermont, where it is more affordable.

I often cringe when I hear someone has bought an old house and is remodeling. I understand that homes need paint and repairs. I realize they need modern appliances and new windows and doors. But why add all the upgrades, such as marble and granite, raising the standard of living to levels that are out of reach for regular families?

There are other ways we can spend far more than we should. At certain holidays like Valentine's Day and Mother's Day, flowers are given to the sweet lady of the house. The stores carry roses for as much as $60 or more. Our local floral department also carries lovely bouquets of carnations for less than $5. I have to ask. . . which flowers would you want? I made a mistake one year. I was offered any flowers I wanted. I could not help craving the large $50 display of pink roses. They were beyond my means and something I have never been able to have. There were many alternatives, which were just as lovely - including $5 or $10 options. But I kept looking at the pink roses. Just once, I thought, I would love to have the rich ones. They were happily purchased for me and I took them home. I loved them, but I would have been happier with the less expensive ones. After the initial shock of having them on the parlour table, I started to dislike them. What an extravagance! The waste of money (that we could not afford to spend) is what bothered me more than anything else. I would be just as happy with pretty daisies, lilacs from the garden, or simple carnations. I learned my lesson.

I know of a family, with a modest income. They recently spent hundreds of dollars in birthday gifts for the wife. Not long after that, they struggled financially. They did not expect car repair bills or an extra high heating bill. They got into trouble because they lived above their standard of living. I suggested they set a yearly limit on gifts, to perhaps $20 to $50 for each person as a maximum. Those gifts, carefully selected, will bring just as much happiness, while keeping funds available, at a steady pace, for the common needs that come up in life. When we figure out our means on a yearly basis, we can set our personal standards and stick with them.

In the old days, of the 1800's and early 1900's, they would define "extravagances" as trying to live in society. It was attempting to live outside of your financial means - to be something you were not. The very wealthy were said to be the most important people. To live among them, to be invited to their social events, meant that you were moving up in life. You had to have money to dress a certain way, to live in a fashionable house, and to eat dainty and abundantly rich food. This cost a great deal of money. Yet, even then, there were happy families who lived quiet lives in common villages. They did not have social ambitions. They were happiest in their humble homes and with a dedication to character, virtue, family, and a life dedicated to trust and faith in the Lord.

Our standard of living dictates what we are comfortable with, in life. For the very wealthy, who know no other way, it can be living the high life, or one of charitable service. For the middle and lower financial classes, we live more simply. We would not dream of spending over our means. This only brings debt, trouble, and unhappiness. There are so many choices in our way of life, in the homes we choose, the food we buy, and the presents we give, that we can choose a simple standard of living that brings just as much happiness as those living in riches. I will venture to say, that many who have a simple standard of living are more content in life. They are less spoiled, less selfish.

A simple life can be such a beautiful thing. There is a quiet grace and gentleness to a basic standard of living. There is no want. There is little need. It is contentment beyond measure. We have to remember that this world is not our home. There are mansions waiting in Heaven. We are pilgrims passing through this way, but once. Living with eternity in mind will bring the greatest happiness of all.

"Our fair morning is at hand; the day star is near the rising, and we are not many miles from home. What matter, then, of ill-entertainment in the smoky inns of this worthless world? We are not to stay here, and we shall be dearly welcome to Him to whom we are going." - Samuel Rutherford, 1600's -

3
Don't Forget the Cheetos, Me`me

I was having a little problem with food. Some of the grandchildren have such good appetites that they eat a great deal during their visits here. They have snacks, lunch, more snacks, and sometimes even dinner. They often help me make all the food. During their visits we also do projects and play in the nursery room. We have such a precious time. It is fun to be at Me`me's house.

But when their Mother says it is time to go home, the children run to my kitchen and need more food. They want bags of crackers, apple slices-to-go, another muffin, or whatever they happen to see. One day, I had bought a bag of those "simply Cheetos," which is a sort of healthier version of the regular brand. The children spotted this exciting snack and wanted an entire baggie full, each, before they left. I knew they would be back the next day and I was running out of treats. So, this is what I did:

I held the bag of Cheetos in my hand. I had each of the four babies line up in front of me, by their age. It was to be the oldest (age 6) to the youngest (age 2). They happily complied. This was fun! Then I told them: – Each would be given only one Cheeto. They were to say "thank you." I would say, "You're welcome," and then they were to walk over to the door to stand with Mama. You should have seen how cute they all looked. They loved it.

We did this the next day, and the next, until it became the routine. There they would be, all with their coats and boots on, lined up by age. I would announce, "Do you know what you are supposed to say?" Little 4 –year old grand-girl, second in place, would lean out of the line and whisper, "I know what to say." Then she would lean back in.

Each day, I would keep coaching them to say their lines, "I am going to give you this Cheeto," I would tell the 2-year-old. He would nod his little head. "Then you say, 'Thank you, Me`me'," I told him. "Then you walk over to the door." He says, "okay," happily takes the Cheeto, says his line, and finishes his part. Each child does this perfectly at every visit. It only costs me four Cheetos. They all love it.

One day, after a very tiring visit, I was sitting on the couch, not paying attention. The children were in their coats and boots. Grand-girl noticed I was not going into the kitchen as usual. She held her little toy puppy and said, as they were getting ready to leave, "Don't forget the Cheetos, Me`me." I jumped right up and got them. It has become such a precious part of our visits.

4
Spring Housekeeping in Winter

I have not been feeling well for some time. The winter has been long and harsh and has kept me a shut-in. I have ventured outdoors only a few times since last December. The bitter winds, below zero temperatures, and blizzard - like snowstorms have been frequent. I have remained cozy and occupied indoors. It has been pleasant and lovely to keep busy with the winter home arts. But as the days wore on, I started to feel sluggish, tired, and just not right. Even my daily exercise program was not helping me feel better.

Yesterday it was a sunny, mild day. The early afternoon temperature was around 30 degrees. It almost felt like spring! While we still have 10-foot snowbanks and plenty of snow all over our property, here in Vermont, the bright sunshine and quiet air was inviting.

I decided to open windows. I wanted to air out the rooms. Our wood stove had just gone out. It was the perfect time to act. Fireplaces and stoves cannot run constantly. We have to let them go out so the ashes can be cleaned out. The rooms are often still warm, from the lingering heat, for quite some time. Then, when a bit of a chill begins to enter, the fires are set to blazing, once again, for our comfort.

At this hour, there was a quiet brightness to the day. There was no wind or chill. I started opening windows. The fresh, winter air gently filled the house. It crept in slowly with little notice. I started to feel my health reviving! The house was in desperate need of fresh, clean oxygen. This was something I should have been doing on a more regular basis.

We cannot open windows on windy, bitter days. We cannot air out the house during a blizzard. But between storms, and on quiet cold days, we ought to open windows for short periods of time, in order to freshen up the house. This affects our overall health.

I started to feel so well that I wanted to clean my son's room. (He is in his 20's and works full time.) He is the only one of our five children still living at home. Before he left for the afternoon, I told him I would be airing out his room and doing a little work. He thought that was good. Soon I opened the windows and dusted window sills. Then I thought I would wash his bedding and surprise him by doing some of his laundry. Normally he does his own cleaning and laundry, but I wanted to do the work on this afternoon.

I came up with organizing ideas for his clothes, straightened the sofa he has in his large room, and organized papers and bookcases. I removed empty boxes and packaging that were waiting by the stairs to be discarded. While the beautiful winter air crept into his room, I turned on a little lamplight and made the room look homey. I thought of every little thing I could do for his comfort. The entire floor was thoroughly swept, trash was removed, the bed was made with fresh bedding, and pillows were tidied and made neat. I did this all - here a little, and there a little, throughout the afternoon, as I

Homemaking for Happiness

needed many breaks. I also took a great deal of time to stop and visit with my husband. He was telling me stories and making me laugh. Then we would both go back to doing our own home projects. It was like taking little tea breaks with Mister. Somehow the room seemed to clean itself!

A chill began to invade the house. It was time to shut all the windows. The sunny spring-like day was replaced with the reality of winter. My husband lit the fire on the stove. Our warmth and comfort returned.

Late that evening, I heard my son return home from work. I wanted to see his reaction to the work I had done. I pointed out some of the things I did so he could find his belongings without any trouble. He looked at the freshly made bed, the bright, clean, organized room and was so happy. As I started to leave the room, he quietly said, "my sweet little mother." He was grateful and happy to be home.

This is the beginning of spring cleaning. It has been such a precious time of keeping house.

5
A Surprise Supper

There have been some changes to the menus here in my kitchen. My husband suddenly decided that he would not eat meat. He didn't want dairy, eggs, or any animal product. This was a complete shock because he never could understand why I stopped eating meat 22 years ago. I did this because I had cancer and was in a crisis. I ate a simple diet of fresh fruit, vegetables, oatmeal, etc. But I would not eat meat, not even chicken soup. According to my research (all those years ago) when the body is in crisis, you eat the purest, healthiest food in order to heal. It took me about 6 years to feel like I fully recovered from cancer. Since then, I have added cheese, eggs (for baking recipes only), and some processed food back into my diet. What made my husband suddenly change his diet? He had watched a documentary!

The first several days, I was so stunned I did not know what to feed him. He realized he needed to compromise so he added dairy and eggs back into his diet. I missed making him beef stroganoff, chicken fettuccine alfredo, and all the other things I had always made for him. Even though I did not eat meat, I have continued to make it for my family. Very often, I would sit at the table with a delicious salad, while the family was served homemade beef stew. I have been doing this for more than 20 years and have been very happy with our routine. But with him changing his diet, I had a great deal of trouble figuring out what to feed him. A man cannot live on salad and oatmeal!

One evening we had pancakes. Another evening we had mashed potatoes and peas with bread – my favorite meal. (I was feeding him the things I normally ate alone.) We were running out of groceries and I had to invent something for dinner. I told my husband I would call him to the table in 30 minutes. Supper was to be a surprise. I set the table with a pretty tablecloth, candles, and my pretty dishes. Napkins and silverware were at each place setting. The poor man was so hungry and had no idea what I was making.

The candles were lit; the lighting was dim and cozy. I called out that "Supper is ready." I loved seeing the look on his face when he realized I had made him a cheese pizza! He was delighted! This was his surprise supper and he was so thankful.

Not long after this, he realized it is okay to eat meat in moderation. He has starting making hamburgers on the grill and is eating beef stroganoff again. I am relieved! The good that has come out of this menu crisis is that he is making the effort to eat more fresh and natural foods, for which I am so grateful!

6
The Little Jobs of Spring Cleaning

When we think of the annual cleaning, some may get overwhelmed. They think they must deep clean the entire house in a matter of a few days. This is enough to stress us all out and nearly give up. But the basic work of spring cleaning, really only consists of two little jobs.

The first, and most important job, is to thoroughly clean all the windows from the inside. This is vacuuming out the window sills, polishing the glass, cleaning the frame, and (if at all possible) hosing down the screens. Then someone ought to clean the windows from the outside. We need these windows completely spotless because so much dirt and dust has accumulated over the winter season. When spring comes, we want fresh, clean air to enter our homes. We do not want that air mingled with dust or germs. We want a clean, fresh home, and that starts with clean windows.

The second job is cleaning the porches, steps, and outdoor entryways. We get these good and swept, ridding them of any cobwebs, dust, dirt, and clutter. We should do some weeding and a little light landscaping to get the area ready for the season. Cleaning these areas is important because they have been neglected all winter long because of snow and ice. A good clean porch, tidy steps, and a polished entryway helps keep the area clean for all who enter the house. This also helps keep the house clean.

The reason we do not need to deep clean the entire house at this time, is because a weekly deep cleaning should occur all year long. We should be washing the floors each week. We should be vacuuming and dusting each week. We should be cleaning light fixtures regularly (whenever needed or monthly). The refrigerator should be cleaned weekly. The bathroom should be thoroughly cleaned each week. All the deep cleaning is done throughout the year to maintain a clean and sanitary home.

If the weekly work seems overwhelming, remember to eliminate clutter and keep things organized. We should have a day each week devoted to organization because things are constantly added to our homes. Emilie Barnes always had such good books on keeping things organized. This will make the deep cleaning so much easier. Spring cleaning should be an exciting time of anticipation. Clean porches and sparkling windows tell us that the cheerful season has begun. We will enjoy beautiful clean air and lots of sunshine. It is an exciting work that will bring us a great deal of joy.

7
Easter Morning

I got up extra early today to get an apple pie in the oven. I need it to bake, and then cool for 2 hours, so I can wrap it up before I leave for Church. We are having some of the family over this afternoon for Easter. We will have pie and ice cream. I am also serving easy, buffet style, food to make things very simple.

Since it is Passover week, I also have to make a very quick batch of unleavened bread. Our local stores, for some reason this year, are not selling anything of the kind. I have always been able to purchase plenty for many years. But not this year. So, I am making a very simple batch and it will only take a few minutes. Then we will have the unleavened bread on hand, which is such a precious part of the season.

I have been very ill off-and-on for several weeks now. But I needed to drag myself out of bed and "Make an Easter for the Family," as Connie Hultquist would say. I will be okay. My husband (who is disabled) and I learn to live in pain and suffering. He will say that he is going to suffer whether he is doing something in life, or sitting still and hurting. He chooses to do things and live, rather than do nothing and suffer. He will suffer no matter what. But we put on a happy face and enjoy the family, and our home, and all the wonderful blessings we have.

Some of the grandchildren will be here this afternoon. I love when they visit. They require an enormous amount of work, but it is the greatest work of all. I love their smiles and laughter and their happy visits.

Some of us will be going to church this morning. I had been home most of the winter and have not been to church from January, of this year, until the beginning of April. The bitterly cold, icy, Vermont weather was unbearable and unsafe for me to venture out. So, I am extra thankful to be able to attend services. I may have to bring my cane for extra support when I go to the service today. I am completely exhausted and drained. (Last week I was shaking in church, I was so tired.) But I do have 2 of my grown sons, who will be with me, and they will be dressed in their suits and looking very handsome. I call them my bodyguards. It will be a joy to go, whether I need a cane or not. And, of course, I can have a good long rest later in the day.

I was reading about old - time street vendors who sold Easter lilies and I thought how pretty that would be to have some beautiful flowers today. It is a joyful time!

8
A Comforting Sick Room

One of the most important things to learn, in homemaking, is how to set up a sick room. Sometimes a patient is bedridden for a couple of days. This can get dreary and depressing without pleasant care. The patient may be a young child or an elder. This family member is receiving special care in their own home. The housekeeper can do many things to make the sick room a pleasant place for both the patient, and the family.

I was chatting with an elderly relative recently. We were talking about the trials of sickness and also of those in constant pain. She told me that, years ago, nursing homes were not common. She remembered an Aunt who lived in a "sick room" off the kitchen of the family home. She said, in those days (before the 1960's), it was common for the sick to be cared for at home.

I did a brief bit of research on this and found a description of a nursing home (on one of the American government sites). It described the nursing home as a place for those who need help, in daily life, but have no one at home to care for them.

My grandparents lived with us when I was growing up. Grandmother was in a wheelchair and bedridden. My mother was in charge of her daily care, as well as the care of our household and family. When I was very young, my mother would need to go to

Grandmother's room, to spend time with her, or to render some service. Mom would telephone her sister and sit me in a chair. She would hand me the phone. My Aunt kept me busy talking, so Mother could manage the sick room without having me underfoot.

Everyone in the family had a part in helping, whenever someone was in need of care. It builds character and gives us all the opportunity to do good deeds. It helps build strong families when this is done with willing and cheerful hearts.

Perhaps there are many, these days, who did not grow up seeing the labor of tending an old - fashioned sick room. It can be a work of cheerful benevolence. I wanted to share some ideas on providing a pleasant room for those with a brief illness.

For the comfort of the patient, it is nice to offer such amusements as word search puzzles, books, and even old-fashioned television programs to make one laugh.

My mother was a wonderful nurse, even though she had no formal training. She would take gentle care of a sick child, settling him in bed during an illness. She would bring in a tray for meals. There would be a little table or desk, beside the bed, for the thermometer. There was even a little bell for the patient to ring for help. Lots of pillows and cozy blankets were brought into the room.

Mother kept a supply of *essentials for sickness* in a bedroom closet. This consisted of bottles of ginger ale and boxes of jello-mix, hidden away where the family could not use them as common treats. She never had to run to the store when an emergency suddenly occurred. There was always chicken in the freezer. She would start to defrost this and make homemade soup the next day. The patient would be served delicious, nourishing chicken soup for days. She would add a little rice, carrots, or delicate pasta to this as the patient began to improve.

Mother also kept anti-nausea medicine and pain relievers in a cabinet, along with bandages, and hydrogen peroxide for first - aid treatments. She had an ice pack in the freezer to handle bumps or sprains. There was an ace bandage, stored away, in case it was needed.

For the patient who is contagious - with the flu or a terrible cold - they would not be allowed visitors in the room. They would be given a wet cloth to cool a feverish forehead. If they are not able to get up each day, Mother would bring in a basin of warm water and soap. She would take a cloth and wash the face and hands. This would help the patient to feel neat and comfortable.

For those suffering for a time, of pain, an injury, or from weariness, when a patient must be in bed, it is so nice to have the family stop in for short visits throughout the illness. The room should be kept as pleasant as possible. The room could be aired by opening widows for a short time, while the patient is in another room. The sheets should be freshly washed. A neat and clean room will help bring happiness.

When Mother is the sick one, she could do her hair and makeup and put on a clean nightgown. This boosts her mood and makes it pleasant for those who visit her. During the times I have been bedridden from an illness, I have often had my children come in to read the Bible, sing hymns, make me laugh, and just tell me about their day. I enjoy using the telephone for short visits with grown children, especially during a sickness. Older children will stop in to see me, for a cheerful visit, before they head off to work or to some errand. I recently suffered from an illness that was exhausting and required a great deal of rest. It was such a blessing to have a pleasant room to enjoy during recovery.

The sick room could be one's own room, a guest room, or whatever bedroom is most convenient to the kitchen. It should have cheerful curtains, soft lamplight, and peaceful decorations to help one recover from one's suffering. There ought to be a chair for guests and a handy tray - table for meals and tea. Fresh sheets ought to be available, both before a patient enters, and after they have recovered. After the occupant is well, the room needs to be thoroughly cleaned, aired, and disinfected, and put back "to rights."

Sickness and injury comes to all homes, in all generations. This is a precious time for prayer and ministry. It can draw our hearts near to God. Our gentle service, in caring for our family during these difficult times, can be accomplished with grace, patience, and love.

"We have no right to murmur at sickness, and repine at its presence in the world. We ought rather to thank God for it. It is God's witness. It is the soul's adviser. It is an awakener to the conscience. It is a purifier to the heart. Surely, I have a right to tell you that sickness is a blessing and not a curse, a help and not an injury, a gain and not a loss, a friend and not a foe to mankind. So long as we have a world wherein there is sin, it is a mercy that it is a world wherein there is sickness."— J. C. Ryle, 1800's.

9
Neglecting the Housework

I was so tired the other day that I spent most of the time resting. While it is essential to rest, it is not okay for me to be a slacker. I enjoyed several hours of reading, watching old black-and-white television programs, and puttering through a few minor homemaking tasks. This was a much-needed day of rest for me. But sometimes I take resting too far. If I lounge too much, I forget to do the daily housework. I suddenly realized that no one was going to make dinner for me. If I wanted some brownies, I had to bake them myself.

I had to get up the courage to do the work. We all get tired. We all suffer from aches and pains. It is important to rest and take breaks, but we also have to take the time to keep house. I told myself something I often say when I am giving-in to being tired, "*toughen up!*" I already had sufficiently rested. I needed to do the little tasks of home keeping.

Brownies and dinner do not just appear; someone has to make them. By late afternoon, I was able to get into my kitchen and do some real work. I baked and then did some cleaning. I also made dinner. This gave me the strength and energy to get back to normal. I had rested enough, and was so happy to have done some work.

This reminded me of how easy it would be to reduce my standards of a tidy and sanitary home. I could easily neglect washing floors, vacuuming, sweeping, and putting away the laundry. Over time, this would cause me to have a neglected and unhappy home.

An unkempt home may cause sickness and disease throughout the family. This can spread to those in the community. I have read that many diseases, or illnesses, from the past have been greatly reduced in frequency - some have just about disappeared (such as scarlet fever). The reason given is that improved living conditions - in the form of clean homes and good nutrition - have helped prevent these types of sicknesses.

This reminds me how essential it is to have an education in home economics. We should know how to clean and make healthy food. We should know how to manage a home. But this takes time to learn. We should be constantly practicing these skills, and continuing to learn, so our families will have a safe and healthy home.

I used to read cleaning books by Don Aslett. I loved his approach to cleaning. Some of his books had cartoon illustrations that were so amusing. He even wrote books about getting rid of clutter. But the sweetest lessons on organizing will always be found in the old books by Emilie Barnes. Her gentleness and faith in the Lord shined through her words and made her readers want a lovely, peaceful home.

I love to see the whole family helping to clean and cook. It is wonderful for them to be involved in all aspects of homemaking. It is important to involve the children in this. Some of my grandbabies think cleaning and baking is part of the fun of their visits to our Estate. I delight in the work, and they catch on to this love and want to be involved.

I appreciate having a routine schedule to follow for days of the week. This way, the plan is already in place. I don't have to think about what I should be doing each day. It would be easy to procrastinate, and avoid work, if we did not have a plan, or goals, for housekeeping. To stay on track, some keep lists on their refrigerator. Others may use 3 x 5 index cards to stay organized. Many use a homemaking binder, where a careful plan of managing one's home is all written out and easy to follow.

The greatest way I have learned to avoid neglecting housework, is to take many breaks throughout the day. There should be tea times (or coffee breaks) and little walks. There should be time for reading storybooks to little ones. A serving of cookies, or a fruit plate, while reading a pleasant book are wonderful times of rest.

In the middle of all this time of recreation, we stop and do a chore. We may do the dishes for 10 minutes before we read. Or perhaps we wash the kitchen floor and then go outside to pick flowers. Housework is easier to manage when there is much time of peaceful rest.

10
The Secret to a Happy Home

There are many ideas for having a happy home. We could always use encouragement in getting along with others, following a housekeeping routine, and of managing money. There are so many good things which will help us have peace and a strong family. But there is one little piece of advice I want to give you. It is the secret ingredient to a happy home. It is this: Don't Panic!

When Mom or Dad are moody, things can get difficult. If the children are not listening, or are causing trouble, it can be stressful. When sickness or financial trials hit, there can be a sense of fear. But if we have some tools in place to handle a crisis, we will not panic.

Years ago, when I was in CPR training, I was shocked at how slow and peaceful the medical staff were in handling a crisis. I have also been a patient at the hospital many times and needed specialized care. But everyone was calm through it all. I have a family member who is a trained Medic, and EMT, and there is never panic. The reason is that they know what to do! Why should they fear when they have training and ways to manage all these troubles? This is why they do not panic.

I want to transfer this idea to the home. The wife is the one who most commonly has the training in home economics. It is more than just cleaning, cooking, baking, and sewing. It also includes family dynamics. It teaches how to get along with others, how to manage children, and how to have a happy marriage. These are the most essential aspects of home economics! We must constantly be learning how to manage relationships. People are always going to be moody. There will be moments of anger and of sadness. There will be mistakes, and there will be regrets. This is life in an imperfect world. No home will be free of trouble. This is why mothers need tools to manage our days, and to remain peaceful and calm through it all.

I would like to share just a few suggestions in getting along with others in the home. I hope some of this will give you some ideas, or inspiration, for your own situation:

1. Marriage:

When a husband comes home from work, he really needs time to relax and not worry about anything. My mother used to get off the phone, or stop visiting with neighbors, whenever Dad came home. This was family time!

They would spend some time sitting at the table with coffee and just visit together and enjoy some peace. Then Mother would start dinner while Dad went to the recliner to watch a little television. But consider this - Dad had Mother's full attention at this time. She was not distracted or busy with outside cares. This showed consideration and respect. They both cared enough about each other to take the time to sit together and just focus on home life.

These days, there are more things taking Mom's attention. There are computers, cell phones, and social media. Just like my Mother would get off the phone, or stop visiting, at a certain time of day, we might consider doing the same with our modern technology. When Dad comes home from work, or when the dinner hour is approaching, it is good to just focus on the family. This will help bring peace and happiness.

2. Teenagers:

When children are young, we expect them to get into trouble, to argue, and to need constant supervision. This is common and normal. But when they get to be teenagers, we sometimes expect them to have the wisdom and maturity of a 50-year-old. We can often be shocked by their behavior. This can cause us to panic. The best tool we can have for this is to set up house rules. Everyone should know what to expect in a household. It is easier to have peace and happiness if we all know the rules. But also realize that new rules can be added as situations come up. Sometimes, we have no idea what is going on in the modern world of teenagers and need to set up boundaries to protect our home life. We can evaluate and change rules as needed. But always remain firm and kind. It is so much easier to point to a chart of rules, than to always be in conflict about every little offense.

As children grow up, they are changing. They are going to have moods and moments of anger. We should practice the art of patience, grace, and mercy. My mother had an incredible sense of understanding. She could get along with anyone. But she was never walked on. Nobody could change her mind about her convictions. She always had incredible dignity, class, and manners, through every trial.

3. Conflict:

We all have heard the Biblical wisdom, "A soft answer turneth away wrath." (Proverbs 15:1). When a family member is angry, know that this is an irrational mood. Anger will pass. It needs time. But a soft and kind answer will help soothe the wrath. This can be simple sentences, such as, "I am sorry this is happening." Or, "I know this is difficult." Then perhaps go back to whatever you were doing. People need time to calm down. When the anger has passed, a normal discussion can happen to resolve future difficulties. I don't know of anybody who can use good manners, or think clearly, when they are consumed with a bad mood. When someone is in an irrational mood, they are not reasonable. There is an old saying that people need time to "cool off."

When trouble happens with a small child - they often throw tantrums because they get overtired or do not know what is best. If we give them a scornful look, they will get more upset. We do not want to provoke our children to wrath. But we can give them a compassionate, loving look. They just want Mom to "make up with them." Mom can make it okay again, with a kiss and a laugh and a letting the moment go. We cannot hold grudges or expect children to be perfect.

Teenagers and small children do not need to get in trouble for every single offense. We are all flawed. Let the little things go with compassion and understanding. Love overlooks imperfection. This is why a set of rules for the home will make it easier to know what is expected. You also want a household routine, or a schedule, so everyone knows when the meals are served, when the chores are to be done, and when bedtime is to happen. With order and routine, there is peace.

Make it easy for others to cheer up, to calm down, and to forgive, by your sweet response. Pride is a powerful thing and can make it very difficult for people to let go of conflict. When Mother makes the effort to restore peace, or give them time to cheer up, she will help restore happiness in the home.

4. Never Make Decisions when you are Emotional:

So many homes have been wrecked, or destroyed, because someone got so mad, or depressed, that they gave up in the middle of a crisis. We have to seek peace. We have to let the emotion calm down. It is like the raging ocean during a storm. We do our best to survive through it. Then when the storm is over, there is a calm and a peace which is restored. This is the only time to make serious decisions - when the fluctuating emotions have settled down. A family, and a home, need to seek constant restoration through each trial. We see problems and we look for ways to prevent them. We repair the holes in a sinking ship, we do not abandon the ship.

5. Don't Be too Busy:

It is essential for Mothers to get rested during the day. This includes avoiding technology, phones, television programs, and thinking about bills. She needs her mind to rest. If she is overloaded with too much going on, or too much to think about, or too much drama, she cannot get through the common trials that occur in the home. She needs to take breaks and to have quiet times for the mind.

6. "Turn Your Eyes Upon Jesus":

This is a favorite hymn. I often sing this song to cheer up and get me through the day. Our trust and our faith, for all things, is in the Lord. This will bring us the greatest rest and joy that others may never understand. Keep reading the Bible (especially the Psalms) and praying each day. Keep seeking holiness and the joy of a close walk with the Lord. This peace that you receive will radiate to those in your household and bless your home.

There are many other ideas we can all come up with to keep our homes happy. But just remember the most important one of all - Do not panic! Every single person is flawed. Every single home has trouble. This is why we should constantly learn (and practice) to be peacemakers, to bring cheer, and to provide a haven of rest for our precious families!

11
Checking on the Gardens

Each day I have been walking the property to check our gardens. Papa planted some cucumbers out front, in little plots near the old wooden wagon. I love to see their progress each day. Right beside this section there are lilac bushes. These have the most delightful scent and are so pretty to see.

Slowly I walk towards some little wild flowers along the edges of the land. There are tiny blue ones and delicate white ones. These come up every year. I notice my tulips did not flower this year. They will have to be replaced this fall. Then I walk over to our apple tree. This does not do much. There is little change since we planted it a few years ago. I don't think it will ever produce apples, but I am always hopeful, as I look at the bright green leaves that are growing. The apple tree is my experiment in seeing if it will do anything, despite my neglect.

Next, I visit the blueberry bushes at the back of the property. These are lush with green leaves. They always produce some fruit for us each year. I never stop being surprised when I get some fresh blueberries from them.

One afternoon, Papa walked with me to visit our strawberry garden. I keep saying I need to do some weeding. But as we stood there, looking at all the flowering plants and seeing how well they were doing, Papa said, "Don't weed them this year." He smiled at me. "I think they will do better if you don't touch them." We both laughed. It looks like we will get a good crop with my neglect.

My little garden walks give me a great deal of peace and happiness. One of my dreams is to have white roses planted in front of our porch – just elegant white roses. I also want white daisies in different parts of the property. I think this will be so pretty to have. I tell Papa about my flower dreams. I know he is the only one who can plant and help everything to grow. When we garden together, it is just him doing the work while I watch. I enjoy the visits to the garden and the idea of gardening, but I just cannot bring myself to do much more than that. I find a great deal of joy in just walking around the property each day.

12
Difficult Times with the Family

All homes have their good times and bad ones. We do our very best to make good memories and have happy times. During the storms, we have to find some comfort to get through them. This is especially difficult when we are talking about adult children who are struggling in life. Perhaps they are making poor decisions that are bringing painful consequences in their lives?

There are two things, in particular, that can make life much harder for adults. One is, taking on debt when one is already broke. For those who have a time of limited income, one can either be broke and free (or peaceful), or one can be broke with extra debt. This extra debt is often taken on repeatedly, in cycles, to keep trying to get more money. This kind of broke (with debt) is misery because one is constantly under pressure. So, when we are struggling financially, we will be broke either way. But if we choose to avoid constantly taking out loans, or borrowing money from everyone, we will not be stressed. Isn't it better to be broke and free (or peaceful)?

Another example, is when one is so upset, or struggling with trials, that it affects them emotionally. This can come to a point where they seek comfort in the wrong things – such as alcohol or dangerous living. This behavior does not improve the situation – it only brings destruction, causing more harm to one's life. In both cases, whether it is money, or destructive living (or anything else that is harmful), the person is seeking relief and comfort in the wrong places. They are not able to fix their situation, or get back on a good, solid path, because their way of living is extremely harmful. In both cases, if we have genuine faith and trust in the Lord, we will find our comfort. This is what will get us through those trials – prayer, Bible reading, listening to good sermons and hymns, and giving the burdens, worries, and painful emotions to God to handle for us.

It sometimes takes many years for adult children to learn these lessons. When mothers and grandmothers watch our children go through these types of things, we have to be so careful not to let sadness, or hurt, ruin our own lives. We cannot be dragged down into despair, along with the struggling one. We have to find some extra comfort in the Lord to help us, as we watch the painful lessons our children are learning.

When this type of thing is happening around me, there are a couple of books I take out of my home - library to read. One of the most important ones, to me, is *"Lena"* by Margaret Jensen. She is the beloved author of *"First we Have Coffee."* (Margaret was born in 1916. And this book, *"Lena,"* was published in 1985.)

Margaret had a wayward, grown son, and to quote part of the description from the book, it says, "Margaret's spirit struggled with an intense battle between anxiety and faith. But God was quietly at work." It is an incredible story from her own life. It is about how her dear friend, Lena, helped strengthen her faith, and hope, through the difficult days while her son was struggling with the world. It is a comforting, encouraging story! It also helps those mothers who are going through similar days of trouble, to have courage and know they are not alone.

Another book I like to read is called, "*It's My Turn*" by Ruth Graham. It is a small book full of precious stories from her home life. There are adorable moments in her early motherhood years that make me smile. She also had difficult days. On page 131, of this book, there is an incredibly comforting writing called, "*Storms*," that I find to be so precious during the rough times of mothering older children. I know, from other books by Ruth, that some of her five children went through periods of being wayward or prodigal. This happens to so many of us! We have to keep reminding ourselves that these are just the growing up years, and are being used to train and mold our children into what God wants them to be.

We can rest in this and trust in Him to take care of them. Why should we worry? We must keep letting that go and keep giving it back to the Lord through prayer. This is how we mothers can get through those difficult times in the family.

13
Housekeeping with an Injury

For several days I had been busy baking, cleaning, cooking and taking care of my family. Grandchildren were my frequent guests, and I enjoyed all my homemaking duties. But one day, after everyone went home, I started to clean up the lunch dishes. As I walked back towards the kitchen, I had a severe pain in my leg. I could not walk. It was terrible. This was a minor injury that was frustrating. Everyone was either gone, or outside. There was no help at the moment. Somehow, I managed to get to my room and find my crutches. I knew I could finish my work with a little help. It took me a great deal of time to get the precious kitchen work completed, but I wanted to do it! I was so happy to have a crutch to help me get around.

I also have a cane and kitchen chairs. These, along with my crutches, are my special tools to help me do my work when I am sick, injured, or suffering. I can sit by the sink while I wash dishes. I can sit at the table while peeling potatoes or preparing salads. I can use my crutches to maneuver around the kitchen and parlour making things tidy, which brings me great joy.

I knew this was a minor injury and that it would not last. Once my work was finished, I went to my room to rest, prop up my leg with a pillow, and watch "*Little House on the Prairie*" on DVD. This was a wonderful reward for all my hard work.

By the next day, my leg was improved enough that I didn't need the crutches any longer. I still felt some minor pain, but knew it was getting better. Sometimes we are able to do a modified version of our housework. At other times we need complete rest and must rely on others to do our work. But it is such a blessing to have tools available to help us in our homemaking, during those difficult days of dealing with an injury.

14
Restraining Domestic Spending

The beginning of spring is my favorite time of year for buying pretty clothes or something nice to decorate our home. There are always pretty pastels and cheerful designs that are only offered during the Easter holiday. I have been thinking about getting something like a pretty dusty- rose colored, chenille blanket and a matching throw-pillow, trimmed with white lace, to add some feminine charm to our life. I also wanted some lovely fake flowers to add to the beauty of home. But most of all, I wanted to find some pretty, feminine dresses to add to my wardrobe. Spring is the time for me to do all these things, but only if there is money available. I dream about the spring shopping each year. It rarely happens because money is always needed for a more noble purpose – such as food and heat for our home. Money to spare does not come around very often.

This year, the idea of buying pretty things and pretty clothes just does not seem practical, when we must use whatever money is available for extra food and supplies, to get through these uncertain times. I must restrain my domestic spending. We must buy what we need, and be content with what we can afford. If there is extra money, it should be saved for more difficult days.

We are so tempted, in our culture, to buy treats and presents for ourselves and others. Shopping and spending are encouraged as happy recreation. I do think occasional treats are a great blessing, but they must be done cautiously and with restraint. Money must not be wasted. We cannot buy everything we think we want. Our houses would be overflowing with material goods, and there would be no place to actually live! Just like we should not spoil our children with excess, we must not spoil ourselves.

It is important to find other sources of happiness. We can be frugal and prudent with our resources, while trusting the Lord to provide all of our needs. This brings us close to God and gives us contentment and peace. Somehow, the closer one walks with the Lord, the more joy one finds in living on less money. It is the ideal way to live – walking along the path to those heavenly gates. We restrain ourselves from getting caught up in the worldly glitter of things while focusing, instead, on the grace and beauty of eternal matters.

15
The Full Pantry
(March 2020)

Some startling news was circulating throughout our area. It seems there was an unknown illness (a virus) wreaking havoc all over the world. My husband started to panic. He wanted us to go shopping and buy a great deal of food and supplies to prepare for a disaster. At first, I did not understand his concerns. Living in rural, northern Vermont, I am used to stocking up on many things to last us for several weeks. It is hard to go anywhere. There are limited stores around here. If we wanted to go to a shopping mall, we would have to leave the state, or drive 2 hours into the city. Winters are bitter and we are often snowed-in. Car trouble frequently leaves us without transportation and can keep us stranded at home. I was used to making sure we had enough, if it was at all possible. But to make my husband happy, to ease his anxiety, I took some money from our small savings and bought a few weeks' worth of extra groceries.

When I returned home from the supermarket, my sister (in Massachusetts) called to tell me what was happening in her area. Store shelves were being emptied. There was panic everywhere. What she was seeing in her community had not yet come to my state. I was shocked and grateful for her report. We realized we needed more items and began ordering some things online to last us for a longer period of time. We needed to have a full pantry, to wait out this storm of a dangerous virus that was causing many to need to stay home.

It soon became apparent that many items were difficult to find. Many of the store shelves were empty. We made do with alternatives and went without non-essential items. It soon became very startling to even enter a grocery store. There were stickers all over the floor to direct where customers were to stand. Some kind of Plexiglass - partition separated cashiers from customers at the check-out counters. Many people were suddenly wearing makes. All the fun of shopping and buying food had disappeared. A whole new way of life had entered. All I wanted to do was stay home and avoid the stores entirely.

This made me realize how precious it was for grandmother to garden, preserve the harvest, and stock her home with most of the year's supply of food for her family. I wanted a full pantry and to be able to focus more of my time and attention on home and avoiding the shopping. I was grateful for my husband's initial panic that set this in motion. We decided we better order seeds and plants and do a big garden this year, even with our limited experience. It turned into a fun adventure that distracted our minds from the worry of the illness that was looming around the world. We wanted to avoid the plague by staying home. But we wanted to be productive and happy as well. The work involved in gardening, planning, dreaming, and shopping to fill up a pantry – to provide the food we wanted for our family, for a long period of time, is a wonderful work for which we are grateful. It is something that grandmother had been doing all along.

16
What Did You Do Today?

During snowy winter days we are sometimes shut-in at home. There may be blizzards, icy cold, and hazardous driving conditions. These are times when we must stay home. After a few days of rest, we might get into a routine of idleness. This may also happen as we are recovering from some illness or bout of exhaustion. We forget to do little routines of chores that keep us productive.

This month, I decided our household needed a morale boost. Instead of drawing attention to the lack of activity, I wrote a note and put it on the kitchen table. The title was simply, "What Did you Do Today?" I added columns and places to put someone's name. This was followed by a blank row to fill up with whatever activity was accomplished.

I got right to work doing chores and writing down all that I was doing. I even included simple actions that are not commonly noticed, such as, "Opened all the shades and windows," "Made my bed," and "Did the evening dishes." The more little jobs I did throughout the day, the more I was inspired to do a few more.

I put out fresh new paper, each day, to be filled out by anyone who wanted to write down their productivity. After a couple of days of this, I felt my energy and inspiration come back. I was able to keep busy and not give-in to idleness. My little plan worked beautifully.

Did anyone else join me in this project? Each day, I was the only person in our home who wrote on the paper. I noticed some were secretly reading my entries. I also noticed there was more cleaning and activity going on with everyone else in the household. So, while they may not have joined my list, they were certainly inspired to get up and get moving again.

17
Patience and Faith While Staying Home
(March 2020)

There have been incredibly difficult times throughout the generations. We have endured wars, plagues, The Great Depression, storms, and many great losses. Through it all, those who have courage and bravery have endured with a *steady calm* of patience and faith in the Lord.

This morning I was reading from the writings of beloved author, Elizabeth Prentiss. I read some from her life and letters, "*More Love to Thee*" and her book "*Urbane and His Friends*," which has some of her letters in the back of the book. I was intrigued by some similarities of what she lived through compared to our current crisis with the virus pandemic. Her daily life and the care of her home and family, through painful events, is what inspired me. She continued to be a good wife, mother, and homemaker regardless of the suffering she endured.

In 1853, she was shocked by the sudden death of her cousin, Louise Shipman. Miss Shipman had been staying with the family and had become ill. Elizabeth had been taking care of her, with the help of the doctor who made visits to the home. The illness had been sudden and shocking. She described how very dear and blessed she felt to have had Louise there in their midst. She was a sweet and kind girl. Elizabeth described her thus: "Her patience was very remarkable and touching. I never saw a sick person so gentle, so considerate, so little disposed to think of self."

Shortly after this, another member of the house, one of her children, became ill. Then her brother, who had been visiting, became ill. On page 140 of her Life and Letters, it is said that Mrs. Prentiss "became a nurse to them both, and passed the next two months quarantined within her own walls."

Mrs. Prentiss wrote letters and took care of the home each day. She wrote to a friend: "I was very sorry not to see Dr. S., who called with your letter, but I am in quarantine, and cut off from the world." I imagine the friend had "called" by coming to the house and brought the mail, but was not able to see anyone in the house.

Later, in her letters, around 1864 she talks of the national struggle, which is now called (from what I gather) The Civil War. She wrote to a friend: "My spunk has got a backbone of its own and that is deep-seated conviction, that this is a holy war, and that God himself sanctions it. He spares nothing precious when He has a work to do." Yet, news was slow to reach her. She mentioned that she had not had any news for a week. On page 220 of her letters she says, "I know next to nothing about what is going on in the world." Her husband kept up to date with the news and shared his thoughts with her. I am sure the national crisis kept her praying. But she kept on with the care of her family and home. She took long walks with her children, laughing with them, enjoying each day, and took great care of them. They were her life and her focus.

Homemaking for Happiness

In her letters, around this time, she mentioned hearing the dreadful noise of coughing from a soldier, in the neighborhood, who had consumption. Such sadness! In April of 1865 she was shocked to hear of the assassination of President Abraham Lincoln. These were perilous and frightening times in which she lived!

Nearly her entire life she suffered from physical weakness and sickness. She had a frail constitution. Despite this, she strove to live all of her life for the Lord. She is the author of the beloved book, "*Stepping Heavenward*," which has blessed many wives and mothers since its publication in 1869.

I was greatly encouraged from my readings this morning. It was especially meaningful because of the dreadful time of uncertainty we are living through today. But I will say that the constant bombardment of news and reports from the media might overtake our every thought, keeping us in a state of terror and anxiety. Yes, there is a dreadful "plague" hovering around and overtaking many. But this cannot consume our lives. We are aware of our duties to do our part in stopping the spread of this virus. We can do this. But perhaps we should not be spending too much time being updated on the dreadful news going on in our communities and throughout the world. In my Mother's day, she and Dad would watch the evening news at 6 o'clock. It was a once-a-day recap from their local state telling its residents what they needed to know. Then they went back to doing their part of taking care of their family and home. This is what life is all about - the quiet dignity of caring for those in one's own home.

No matter what is going on around us, we would do well to give our cares and worries and fears to the Lord in prayer. We must trust Him who loves us dearly. Then let us get back to the business at hand - of nursing and ministering to those in our own homes, protecting them, cheering them on, with great patience and courage, as we wait out this storm.

18
Make an Effort

It is difficult to do housework or chores when one is overly tired. Sometimes we don't feel like doing what is necessary to maintain a home or to provide good, nourishing meals for the family. It is all work. It takes labor. But I have learned that when I am at my most weary, I have to remember to make an effort.

If I am feeling weak, I might have enough strength to do a little job, like clean out my purse. I will also sit on the floor with a stack of old papers and files to put through a little shredder machine. It makes me feel like I have done *something*, but takes limited effort. This builds energy and endurance. It helps me accomplish things. I take a great many breaks. Then I feel motivated and ready to do a bigger job – such as washing dishes or making dinner.

The small efforts give me more strength to do the harder work throughout the day. If I rest for 15 minutes, I feel ready to scrub the kitchen sink and sweep the floor. Then it might be time for another rest. A great big job like making lasagna or homemade pizza is quite an accomplishment and is done in the late morning hours or early afternoon. If I can accomplish one big job a day – even if it is vacuuming or washing the floor, I feel grateful for my efforts at maintaining our home. I have to have the "will" to remind myself to intentionally get up and make an effort. This helps me avoid the temptation of giving - in to a life of wasting time, doing whatever I want, and avoiding the responsibility of creating beautiful things around me. We must get up and do many little things in a day – many little chores, kindnesses, and good works, in order to provide our families with a happy and pleasant home.

19
Help for Staying Home During the Crisis
(March 2020)

I am amazed at how much has changed over the last several weeks. We are seeing, what experts are calling, a worldwide pandemic. A few days ago, our local schools closed. Our restaurants no longer allow indoor dining. Some have closed completely, here in Vermont. I have been following the news reports, trying to understand as much as possible from the experts, and watching what is going on throughout the world.

I have been on the phone for several hours each day with immediate and extended family members. Some of my relatives in Massachusetts gave me local updates of what they were seeing in their towns. There were empty store shelves and panic. This had not yet hit our area, but now I am beginning to see it here as well. It looks like what is happening in surrounding states, is slowly making its way to mine.

We are told to stay home for at least 15 days, in hopes of stopping the spread of a virus. Government authority, in our states and country, have made announcements of what they need us to do. We are doing our best to follow all guidelines.

I have been confined to my home before, on many occasions, due to health difficulties and also from bitter winter months here in northern Vermont. I am used to trying to make sure we have extra things, on hand, like coffee for Mister, and tea for me. We enjoy having those daily luxuries in life, and hope we are able to continue to do so. I have gone to the market a few times over the last week, or so, to get extra water, food, and other supplies. Now I need to settle in and stay home.

Our local churches have just announced that services are cancelled for the coming weeks. I have never seen anything like this happen before. But I appreciate our Pastors, staying in touch with us through email, and helping to guide us through these difficult times. Their faith, and trust, in the Lord, is inspiring and comforting.

There is a temptation to panic. But I want to suggest an alternative. Most people, right now, are not able to go to work. Their children are not able to go to school. The entire family is home together. This is a good time to focus on the tasks of homemaking, meal preparation, cleaning, and enjoying time together. We should be conserving our resources - learning to avoid the waste of food. This will help us avoid having to keep going out to the store. We want to stay home for the duration, to do our part.

We are blessed to have so many resources online - such as articles and videos, to inspire us in lessons in home economy.

But I also want to mention one very important thing - **please expect there to be annoyances among the household**. We are all flawed! We do not always say or do the right thing. We need grace and mercy in our family relationships. Also, please remember that children - both young and old - will misbehave, cause mischief, and get on one's nerves. **This is normal.** This is life. Mothers are the referees and the coaches to help guide the family out of trouble and into more productive behavior. If you notice junior is acting up, please redirect his attention elsewhere. Do not hold grudges when children do wrong. Do not dwell on their moods. Keep things moving along. Is it snack time? Is it time to do a chore? Is there free play? Try to organize a variety of activities to keep your day on some sort of schedule. This will help lessen the bad behavior in our children.

Mothers, we need to keep up the morale in our homes! We need to be the cheerleaders of courage and hope! Don't let this get us down. We can wake up each morning, and do the task assigned - take care of the home, the kitchen, and the family. Let's work on keeping everyone productive indoors, maintaining our health, getting fresh air into our homes, exercising, cleaning, keeping everyone safe and happy, and doing it all unto the Lord.

Do not take on unnecessary burdens. God is in control. Why should we fear? Let's lean on Him to get us through.

20
I Don't Want to Miss a Blessing

In a biography of D. L. Moody, his son shares passages of his father's letters from his life. His writings help us see how his life was lived and what his character and values were like. In one section of the book, Moody was travelling. He stopped at an Inn and stayed overnight. He did not want to travel on the Sabbath. This was considered a holy day that was to be dedicated to resting in the Lord. It was a time to put aside our work in the world and be blessed with a closeness in fellowship with our Heavenly Father. This was a blessing.

These days, in observation of the culture around us, the Sabbath seems like an ordinary day. The shops are open as usual. People are traveling, doing errands, and transacting business, as usual. There is no indication that it is a holy, set-apart day. Because of this, there is a lack of blessing.

Each weekend, something happens to tempt me to do errands, go to the bank, do a little shopping, or go to some unnecessary place on the Sabbath day. On the occasion that I have given - in to this, the day has lost its sweetness. I end up weary from the activities and do not get to do the lovely, restful activities of a beautiful Sabbath day.

This past week, when one of my grown children had asked for me to do an errand, I found myself saying, with a wistful longing, "I cannot go on the Sabbath day. I don't want to miss a blessing." It has always been such a precious time of quiet reflection of holy thoughts and prayers, surrounded by family. It is a day to put aside the common cares of the world – the thoughts of bills, business, shopping, and heavy labor. It is a day of mental and physical rest in the Lord. I don't want to miss it.

21
Confined to the Second Floor

I had a minor injury this month. Somehow, I twisted my ankle and could not bear to walk much. I spent an entire day, struggling with a growing pain, before I realized I needed to get out my crutches. These are a great help to get me through difficult days.

Normally, I am walking all over this house. There are 2 sets of stairs, with about 15 steps each, connecting the 1st to the 3rd floors. Clearly this type of walking could not happen while using a set of crutches. I was confined to the second floor.

For a great deal of the time, I had to lay down with my foot propped up on a pillow. This provided some relief from the pain. Somehow, I still managed to do some dishes, the laundry, a little sweeping, and to get myself little cups of tea. I learned to use one crutch if I had to walk to the kitchen to retrieve something. This left one hand free to hold my tea, or do the sweeping.

It is more restrictive to remain in one area of the house, but this was something I was used to doing for much of the winter months. My energy levels are so low in winter because I am fighting to stay warm. It wears me out to use the stairs each day. I learn to stay on the second floor, and do without much of my normal routine. I yield to the idea that this portion of home is like a private apartment where I must remain for much of the time. I am thankful for my little kitchen on this floor. There is also the front parlour and my bedroom.

During these difficult times of recovery and confinement, I do a great deal of reading or hand-sewing projects. I have learned, through bouts of suffering and confinement, an incredible sense of gratefulness. I must be content in all things. There is always a way to find peace and joy, knowing the Lord watches over me.

22
Reviving the Prayer Journal

When I was a young wife and mother, I had so many worries and troubles. There were daily struggles for finances, transportation, and getting the things we needed. I had no hope for any of it, except from the Lord. I used to write little prayers in a diary. I would write out the date, and then say something like:

"Our car has broken down again. It will cost $200 for repairs. How will we pay for this? There is no money in the budget. We have no savings. I give this burden to you, Lord. Please help us."

This would be written at the top of the page. The lower portion of the paper was saved to write out the answer and the blessing.

You might wonder how we managed to get by with a broken-down car while we waited for the Lord to help. I will tell you. . . We walked, or gratefully accepted rides from family members to get us to the store, or co-workers helped get my husband to work. It was more difficult, but we got through until the blessing came.

Once the prayer was answered, I would go back and find the page it had been written on, and I would write out the blessing. The answer might have been something like:

"An unexpected job came up for my husband. He was able to do the extra work for a couple of weeks. This money paid for the car repair. Thank you!" (The answer always came about in an unexpected way!)

At other times, the prayers and the worries were so hard to bear. There would be shoes needed for the children. We may not have had enough food. My husband was laid off work or lost jobs and those were the hardest times to manage. I would write down the prayers and the needs and then get back to mothering and homemaking. I would leave it with the Lord. Sometimes he answered those prayers before the end of the day. At other times, I waited weeks. But always the prayers were answered. I learned to depend on God for all things in this way. I learned not to rush out and try to fix it all myself. I gained patience, and faith, and trust, and was greatly blessed with a journal of answered prayers.

Our lives are not to revolve around material things, shopping, and money. The answer to every problem in life is not being rich or having an abundance of possessions. We are to trust the Lord, **working with Him** in faith, works, and prayers. This creates an incredible bond and a closeness to our Heavenly Father. We might say, "How should I manage this?" Or, "Please guide me in this decision." We pray, "Lord, please take care of me. Please help." We say this each day, just like we ask for our daily bread. The Lord cares for the sparrows who have no home. He provides us with incredible beauty in sunrises, landscapes, the chirping of sweet birds, and the stunning display of flowers. There is beauty, in trust and faith in the Lord. He knows all of our needs, in all times. He waits for us to ask and to trust in Him. This is what makes life so precious.

Perhaps this is a good time to revive the old-time prayer journal?

Any notebook will work well for this. It is like a diary of needs and the asking for help from our dear Lord. Then we write the blessings, the answers, and all the ways the Lord, Himself, has taken care of us, His dear children.

We can also look back and read these precious entries so that we will always remember that it is the Lord who has provided, and not we ourselves. He owns the cattle on a thousand hills! He has the power to give and take wealth, as well as life. Oh, there is great peace in putting our very lives in His hands, and trusting Him for each of our numbered days. We are grateful for His goodness and His precious care.

23
Flowers for the Dinner Table

Late last summer, I went on a little journey. We visited the summer home of the Lincoln family. It is an incredible mansion on a large property. The landscaping is stunning. I had such a nice time walking the grounds. It was such a peaceful place to visit.

The family grew their own flowers. These were regularly cut and brought inside to decorate all over the home. There were vases everywhere. Some held the prettiest flowers called, "peonies." We were told that these were planted many years ago, by the family, in the early 1900's. They were well cared for, and are still thriving to this day. Peonies provide elegant decorations for the home. I wanted to grow some here at our Estate.

Within several weeks of my visit, I asked my husband if we could order some peonies to plant in early fall. I searched around to see if any were available at an affordable cost. It soon became clear that they were out of our budget. I tried to see if the expense would work, but we did not have enough time to save up before the onset of our harsh winter season. It was a frivolous impulse and I had to remind myself that all good things take time.

This spring, we were able to order one "root" of a pink peony variety. It was planted at the very beginning of our spring season, which, here in northern Vermont, occurs at the end of May. My husband and I walked all over the property trying to find just the right place. "Remember," I told him. "These may very well last for 100 years, like the ones at the Lincoln home." He just smiled and humored me (and my dreams).

I knew it was better to plant in fall, but wanted to try a spring planting, just in case it worked out. I was quite impatient! I also understood that peonies could thrive despite my neglect. I expected them to come back (with their beauty), year after year, even in our cold climate. I was so eager to see this lovely plant growing on our very own grounds. It reminded me of the stunning Lincoln Estate that I had loved to visit.

Someday, I dreamed, I would have lush peony plants growing all over our property. I would be able to go out, at our own Estate, and gather these pretty flowers to put on our dinner table. There was a comforting feeling of not having to leave our property to find pretty things to make our home look lovely and inviting.

It did not take long before the plant started to grow. Soon a family of chipmunks made their home under the ground nearby. They had several little babies and were a delight to watch. However, my peony plant started to wilt and did not last long. It may have been a coincident, or perhaps a mild drought contributed to the problem, but I was sad to see the plant fade away. Yet, I will not give up hope. It may revive and return next spring. We also hope to order another plant in the future and keep trying. I will keep dreaming of a property with many peonies, growing on the grounds, to delight our family with pretty things to decorate the dinner table. It is a happy thought. Perhaps someday it will happen?

24
Missing the Lilacs

At my childhood home, in Massachusetts, we had a lilac bush beside the house. I was always so happy when they were in bloom. The scent is so fresh and beautiful. The purple flowers are wonderful to see.

We also have lilacs in Vermont. The season here is so short. I would often go outside and look at them each day. I was afraid to pick them. I wanted to just look at them and enjoy them as long as possible. When my parents lived here with us (for 9 years), my mother used to tell me, "You better pick the lilacs while you can. They won't last long." I started to gather some, every couple of days, for our kitchen table. They made the house smell so sweet. The flowers were simple, but pretty.

This year, I have been very sick and did not have enough energy to go outdoors. I had been waiting for the lilacs to be in bloom. I had been walking outside, as much as possible, just waiting for them to be ready.

One day, when I first started to feel ill, I noticed the lilacs had arrived. I would sit by the window and enjoy the sight, each day. But I was too weak to go outside to pick them. I noticed the bees and butterflies were hovering around the bushes. There had also been a great deal of rain. The lilacs did not last a week. I had missed them for an entire season. There would be no lilacs for me this year. But I am very grateful I was able to see them through the window.

The Lord is so good to provide us with the beauty of nature to enjoy each year. I love things that are familiar and the routines of life. Each season brings us something of beauty, and there is always something delightful to look forward to.

25
Church in the Living Room

There are times, in our lives, when we are not able to attend church in person. We may miss the pews, the song books, the minister, and the people. The church building, itself, is such a wonderful place to be able to go and hear the prayers and listen to the sermon in person. There is such a sense of beauty and holiness in a regular routine of church attendance.

The last few months, we have been having church in the living room. This has become a very precious habit of attending our home church each Sunday morning. We watch America's pastor, Dr. Charles Stanley, and are greatly comforted by his sermons. We may not be able to go anywhere right now, for whatever the reason - the weather, sickness, etc., but we can attend a special service at home.

We have been having a daily Bible time for more than 4 years now, my husband and I. It has made an enormous difference in our lives. Now we have added a weekly church time, together, in the living room.

My husband will call me, at the appointed time, to say that the sermon is all set up and ready for us. I will get my notebook and a pen. Then I will happily walk downstairs to the living room. I have a "journal notebook" which was a gift from In Touch Ministry. It has a ribbon marker and is perfect for taking notes while watching the sermon.

Just before each sermon, I write the date, the day of the week (Sunday) and the name of the message. I then proceed to take notes throughout the message. This has created a record of our "attendance" and faithfulness in doing church at home. We can also see, at a glance, the messages we have already watched, reflect on key points, and be encouraged when looking over the notes. It is easier to remember the lessons when one writes them down. It has been such a blessing to actually see that we have been doing church every single week for months now! It has helped us both very much.

We all need a steady diet of church attendance. We need spiritual nourishment. Our marriages need a regular dose of encouragement. Doing Bible time and Church, together in the home, is a wonderful way to strengthen our faith and stabilize our walk with the Lord.

26
Waiting for the Door to be Opened

It is wonderful to be a peaceful and graceful lady. It is good to have trusted family members to take care of you. Many mothers teach their sons to open doors for girls. They grow up knowing that it is good to protect and take care of the women of the family.

My two grown sons have always opened doors for me. When they were little, I taught them by waiting by the door and looking kindly at them, saying, "Will you open the door for Mother?" It was not long before they were both grown. They are both much taller and stronger than I am. It was not difficult for them to take care of their Mother, by opening doors and carrying heavy items for me. It was a precious way of showing honor and love for me.

Over this last year, I have had to make several trips to stores alone. It wore me out, but was essential work. I am not a strong person and simply do not have the energy, or strength, to do a great deal of labor or lift heavy grocery bags. Whenever possible, one of my grown sons will do the shopping with me so I have the necessary help.

This past week, I remembered a lesson about opening the door for a lady. The day was chilly with drizzly rain. I wanted to stop at a large furniture store, just to look around and to dream. One of my grown sons (in his 20's) was with me. Instead of waiting a few minutes in the car, I was the first to get out and walked quickly to the building. I was in a great hurry to get out of the cold and wind. The door was heavy as I reached it. I did not remember to have patience enough to wait and be taken care of. My son came to the rescue and opened the heavy door for me. I had forgotten that I was not alone and that there was help.

This reminded me of the protection of the Lord. How often do I boldly rush into some idea or decision without waiting for His guidance and help? How often do I ignore the help that is available and wear out my strength and my nerves? How often do I hurry out of some discomfort to get a result, on my own, without consulting the Lord for direction?

The simple act of a lady waiting for a gentleman to open her door produces great patience and a sense of peacefulness. It produces the beautiful virtue of meekness. There is a precious lesson in waiting for a door to be open, with a heart of trust and faith in those who were given to protect her.

May this also remind us that waiting on God to open doors for us, in this life, is how we learn to serve Him and not go our own way. This is how we learn to follow His leading. We are not to be brash or bold. A lady should cultivate the art of a meek and quiet spirit. This is a contented heart who is not in a hurry or a rush to do everything on my own. With a graceful sense of dignity, she yields to wait for the door to be opened. For it is not my will (or my plans) that I want to do, but the will of my Heavenly Father.

27
Old Time Store Clerks

In old literature, I have often read of young ladies (of limited means) who had to work for their living. They were often clerks in a store. One might be in charge of notions and ribbons. Another may be in charge of watches and jewelry. They had long days and little free time. Their income was small, requiring them to live in cheap boarding houses. They hoped and dreamed of, one day, getting married and having a real home of their own.

I recently came across a description of the gentlemen who were also store clerks. In 1882 there was a dry goods store called, "L. S. Donaldson Company." It was located in Minneapolis, Minnesota. They had thirty different departments, including such titles as: "Confections and Fruits;" "Books, Bibles, and Albums;" "Ladies Furnishing Goods:" "Gents Furnishing Goods;" and "Cloaks and Suits." Each department employed clerks to wait on customers.

The Donaldson Company expected their workers to have upstanding moral values and gave a listing of rules for their store. I was surprised to see that they had to work from 6 in the morning until 9 at night. That is a 15-hour work day! The gentlemen were advised that after working 14 hours, they were to spend their leisure hours in reading. They were allowed one night off each week for courting. A second evening off was allowed if they went to Prayer Meeting. The store was closed on the Sabbath day and workers were required to attend church regularly.

I have to admit, I also loved the chores listed that must be done in the store. These included, sweeping, dusting, care of the lamps and chimneys, and the cleaning of counters and shelves. These were daily duties that had to be done, in addition to waiting on the customers. The store had high standards of neatness and presenting their departments in an orderly and pleasant manner.

Our homes and businesses are so different today. The moral character of workers and the standards of living are much altered. There are distractions from television, computers, and endless entertainments, which were not even thought of in the 1800's. How we spend our time affects the development of our characters.

How lovely it would be if we valued old fashioned home life and faithfulness in church. It would be lovely if homes of today had high standards of both cleanliness and a gracious gentility in manners and piety. This would help produce a generation of workers with integrity and morals for our local businesses. Each home and community would be greatly blessed with this old time standard of living.

*Note – Information about the L.S. Donaldson Company, in 1882, was obtained from page 3 of the book, *"Thank You for Shopping: The Golden Age of Minnesota Department Stores,"* published by Minnesota Historical Society Press.

28
Bible School at Home

Many years ago, I learned about education through a pattern of efficiency. I had read the (1948) book, "*Cheaper by the Dozen*" by Frank and Ernestine Gilbreth. They were from a family of 12 children, whose parents worked as efficiency experts. As I read about their domestic life, in a large home, I realized many ways that my own children could learn a great many things throughout a normal day. This was by exposure to good culture, a tasteful home, and having quality educational materials available in the house.

I thought of pretty artwork in the form of charming landscapes, beautiful flower gardens, and old fashioned, welcoming homes. I had a cassette tape teaching the French language and some tapes of peaceful music.

The main part of education, in our house, included lessons from the Bible. We had daily Scripture reading, prayer, and we learned about doing "mitzvahs" throughout the day. These were good deeds and commandments we enjoyed doing with a happy heart. Every little sweet and kind thing we did, we would cheerfully say, "That was a mitzvah!" This type of environment can fill the mind and heart with a beautiful character despite the frailties of our human nature. In all homes, there are bad days, mistakes made, and unkind words spoken, which are later regretted. But the continuous filling up of the home with the beauty of mitzvahs, prayers, and the love of Scripture, brought joy and cheered us along.

This month, as I was teaching homeschool to some of my grandchildren, I noticed a beautiful culture of a precious Bible school in the home. This was at my daughter's house. I teach four of her children, in grades preschool through second grade. In this home, Bibles are visible in the living room. The older children have their own Bibles with little bookmarks of special passages they like to read on their own. They have Bible time with their Mother each day. There is old -time church music playing softly in the background.

I will often hear the children quietly singing along to "*Blessed Assurance*;" "*He Lives*;" and "*Precious Memories*" sung by Alan Jackson. They sing along as they are setting up their school papers, or waiting for me to help them with a new lesson.

On one particular morning, we had our usual time of writing sentences using the current spelling words. Each day, they are required to take four words from their spelling unit and write sentences. On this day, they asked if they could write stories or songs instead of regular sentences. I thought they were going to make things up and wanted to be creative. As they started to write, I was startled to see the 1st grader write the lyrics to a hymn. She had remembered that her spelling words were used in that particular song. I helped her with some of the spelling of the words before I realized what song she was actually writing. Over in the next seat was my 2nd grade student. He was writing out a Bible verse from memory, in his best cursive handwriting, which included some of the words from his spelling list. I was delighted!

I realized that this was what their Mother loved and did her best to live before them in their home. She had helped the children write out Bible verses on construction paper and decorate them to put on the walls. The children practiced their reading as they walked through the house and enjoyed the Scriptures around them. Their Mother's love of the dear Lord reached the hearts of her children, and developed, in them, a very precious pattern of doing mitzvahs and loving the Bible, because that is what is in their hearts.

29
Peace Be Upon This House

I was reading about how the apostles sang a hymn after the Lord's supper. (1) The thought was so precious to me that it gave me a comforting sense of peace. In another passage of Scripture, I read the beautiful words, "Peace be unto you." (2) We are all in desperate need of peace. We need a rested spirit; a contented feeling that all is well... We need peace.

In the home, and in the world around us, there is stress and anxiety. We are often kept on high alert because of conflict, trials, and fear. We are frequently troubled by the actions of others. This can strain our nerves and make us irritable.

Despite all this difficulty, how can we maintain peace in the home?

We ought to think about the peacemakers. These are people who create a happy environment. They provide a place of rest. This allows one to have a time for quiet of the mind. Many homemakers are doing this type of work each day. They continually work on creating an atmosphere of a real and genuine home, where one feels welcomed and safe.

Here are some ideas for helping to calm the nerves and settle into a happy rest at home:

1. To quiet the stressful noise of outside traffic, or the clatter of the noise indoors, it is soothing to turn on a little fan. It blocks the disrupting and sudden sounds around us. The noise of the motor is usually steady and pleasant. I often have a fan going, at certain times of the day. This helps bring peace to our weary nerves.

2. Stop and listen to the rustle of the leaves from the wind. Hear the singing of the birds. Just rest and enjoy the lovely sounds of nature. This is similar to stopping to smell the roses. We look at the beauty around us and it gives us rest. Don't think about your worries - just stop to enjoy the beautiful vision outdoors.

3. To stop the whirlwind of the stress around us, consider how many people try to get away from it all by taking a vacation. They get away from the telephone, the stress of the office, and the city traffic. We can do this (to a degree) in our minds. We can think about walking along a bubbling brook, seeing and hearing the rushing water as it goes along the rocks and land. Or we can find literal ways of resting our minds. This can be as easy at taking the stairs rather than the elevator when in an office building. We can enjoy the walk across the parking lot to get to the grocery store. These extra steps bring quiet and rest to our minds.

4. Minimize the amount of news you are exposed to. We ought to guard the quiet of our minds, much like we guard the peace of little children. We do not need to know everything. Our children need not worry about the troubles in life. Quiet news and peaceful happenings bring cheer. Let us bring cheer to our homes and not spread distressing troubles.

5. Don't be in a rush. It is not healthy to multitask and always be in a flurry of activity. This keeps us too busy to live! When little troubles come, our nerves will not be able to handle anything else if we are too busy. Live a quiet, steady, peaceful life, and you will be ready to calmly face what comes, with the help of the dear Lord (who is with us through it all).

6. Learn to sing the old-time hymns, such as "*Amazing Grace.*" Oh, how much we need the old paths of joyful worship from the heart. When we sing hymns, from the heart, we are comforted and blessed with a quiet sense of joy.

7. Find ways to get along with those in your household. Be a peacemaker. Remember the human frailty of us all. Practice patience and understanding. Give them a gracious love that bears childish days and difficult moods. My favorite hymn, in these moments, is "*Turn Your Eyes Upon Jesus*." It goes on to say, "And the things of earth will go strangely dim. In the light of his glory and grace." This is precious peace!

8. Each time you walk in the door, quietly say these sweet words, *"Peace be upon this house."*

May our homes be little lighthouses of godliness and joy. One of the greatest missions of a homemaker is to have peace in her home.

----

*   1 - Mark 14:26   2 - John 20:19

Summer

{Photograph on Previous Page: A lake, near Mrs. White's home.}

30
Please Use Real Dishes

Some people do not like doing the dishes. They try to make life easier for others by eating on paper plates, a little napkin, or just holding the food in their hands. I am constantly seeing some of my grown children do this whenever they visit. I will make a batch of fresh, homemade muffins. A 20 something – year- old will take two and start to eat while walking away. I call out, "Please use a plate." There are sandwiches that are made and then held in the hand while one is walking through the house. I can practically see the crumbs falling all over. I say, "Don't forget to use a plate."

Cookies and miniature donuts are eaten by grandchildren who wander around their toys as they enjoy their treat. I say, "We need to sit at the table and use a plate."

I love my pretty dishes. Using real plates, and sitting down while one eats, are part of the pleasant things in the home. It also helps keep the house clean. I can easily clean the table, and the floor underneath. But I do not want to hunt crumbs all over the house. One of the little-known tricks, that young people should know, is that it is easier to keep a neat home when one uses real dishes. *I really don't mind washing them.*

31
Travel Budget

A necessary trip to our home state of Massachusetts was suddenly required. There had been a death in our extended family. We needed a strict budget and had to be very careful. Last year we stayed at a campground because we could not afford a hotel. With Papa being disabled, he had suffered very much and we realized our camping days were over. This time, we had no choice but to stay in a hotel. We needed to stay for three nights because the drive was going to be very difficult. We needed extra time to recover.

We chose a hotel a few towns away from where we needed to be. It had the lowest rate in the area. Our stay included free breakfast each morning. They also served coffee and tea at all hours. This would help keep our expenses low.

I told Papa we could manage a spending rate of thirty dollars per day. We bought some of our food from the supermarket and also a few meals at take-out restaurants. I brought fresh baked muffins from home, in a small cooler, to get us through a few days as well. On one afternoon, my father-in-law was having lunch in a beautiful Italian restaurant, right next door to our hotel. He wanted to treat us and we gladly accepted. We had a nice lunch, while visiting. This also helped us save money.

Whenever we have to be away from some of our grandchildren, we want to buy them a little souvenir, or present, to bring back with us. This time, there simply was not any money available. Papa and I went for a short walk on the beach and collected pretty sea-shells for the babies. The walk was peaceful and lovely. It helped soothe our troubled thoughts and brought us happiness.

Now that we are back home, I will have to be extra careful to build up a small savings for a "rainy day."

Journeys and vacations are very expensive. It helps when there is family to stay with. In my childhood days, my Aunt and Uncle would bring their children to visit our suburban Massachusetts' home in the summertime. The only expense they had was the gas money to get to our house. They would pack picnic food for the drive. My Uncle would drive straight through (24 hours), only stopping for gas and rest-stops. When they arrived, they stayed with us and we fed them. On alternate summers, we would go down south to rural Alabama and visit them. Dad also drove straight through. Mother packed our food as well. Our Aunt fed us very well, and was a great cook. We slept on couches, or on blankets on the floor. We enjoyed our Aunt's southern home cooking. These were affordable vacations.

Years ago, I was able to visit my brother and his family in Florida. He fed us and housed us, and we had a lovely time. It is good when we are able to stay with family. When this type of accommodation is not possible, a strict travel budget is essential.

32
Comfort from the Hymn Book

I love reading the songs out of the old hymn book. There are many that I do not know how to sing, but I love to read the words. One of my favorites is *"Sweet Hour of Prayer."* I have heard it many times and we sometimes sing it in church. But I cannot catch it enough to sing it on my own. Instead, I read the verses and find my comfort in the words.

There are several songs that I do know very well. I have the pages marked and folded in my book so I can easily find them. These are the ones that my father sang, throughout the house, as we children were growing up. I heard them so many times that I have them memorized enough to sing them on my own. They are common songs that we also sing in church. These include *"Amazing Grace,"* and *"Just a Closer Walk with Thee."*

I bought a set of hymn books when my children were very young. I think we have 6 or 7 copies of them. I got them from "Sword of the Lord" and I believe the edition I have was published in the 1980's. Each of my five children were given their own copy of the book. Each wrote their own name on the inside cover of their copy. During our daily Bible times, we would get out our Bibles and hymn books and sing together. I still have these books here at home.

It is quite a heritage, started by my grandfather, to sing hymns with the family at home. I am so grateful that my own father taught me many of these old-time Christian songs. One of my goals, each year, is to keep learning the old (and favorite) hymns like "*Sweet Hour of Prayer.*" I find so much comfort and peace in these precious songs.

33
The Slacker and the Messy House

Just before seven in the morning, on a hot summer day, I needed to wash the floors. I started out by cleaning the bathroom. Then I moved kitchen stools, little carpets, toy boxes, and the step -stool, out of the room so I could thoroughly sweep every corner. The last bit of work is to wash all the floors. This is part of my schedule of weekly work. It keeps the house looking pretty and neat. Then I go for a slow, little walk on my treadmill, and listen to a peaceful sermon.

But every week, just before I start the cleaning, nagging thoughts of a slacker enter my mind. I tell myself I am too tired. I say that perhaps I should just sweep and not bother with the washing afterwards? I suggest to myself that a short break would be nice. I practically talk myself out of doing the work until the moment I am finished. This happens every single time I have something difficult to do in the home.

Late this morning, I had to make homemade pizza. I was tired and wanted to sit with a nice book instead. I thought frozen (processed, convenience) pizza, or something else, might be a better idea. Those nagging thoughts of a lazy housekeeper plague me throughout my chores. It is an amusing battle between prudent- and –pleasant-housewifery, and the- slacker- with- the- messy -house.

I decided I would compromise by making the pizza early in the day. It would be all ready and, in the refrigerator, ready to bake at the appointed dinner hour. This way, I could do the work but have much of the evening off to rest. I listened to beautiful hymns on my kitchen radio as I worked.

I have learned to do the hard work while doing pretty and pleasant things at the same time. I will either listen to something peaceful or I will do some happy adventure after the work is finished.

Sometimes I may just take a walk on the grounds to enjoy the fresh air and sunshine. Other times, I will sit in the parlour with a lovely book and some tea. I enjoy accomplishing all the hard work so much more when there is some pleasant reward. The house looks so pretty, and the homemade food is nicely made and served.

I cannot even imagine how messy my house and life would be if I listened to that nagging slacker- of –a- housewife, who is constantly invading my thoughts! It is a daily battle, where I am found smiling and laughing while I ignore that little voice which says, "You deserve a rest. You won't make it through the day if you keep this up!" I would much rather set up a workable plan, doing a few difficult things each day, to bring me great joy and happiness in a pretty home.

34
Simple Days at Home

There is such a thing as a pleasant routine for homemaking. It may seem ordinary to some, or not very exciting to others. But the basic work of housework and of spending time with family is a wonderful way to enjoy our days at home.

Baking in the Kitchen -

I spent the other day baking muffins, brownies, and homemade pizza. The sun was shining brightly through the windows. I could hear the birds singing sweetly, and the rushing sound of the river behind the property. As I worked in the kitchen, the family came in- and- out to get a snack, or to visit with me. I also listened to a precious sermon on my kitchen radio as I was making the pizza. This was the hardest part of my kitchen work - to make the dough and prepare all the pizzas. So, the encouraging sermon was a joy to hear as I did the hard work. It was a blessing!

Playing Games with the Family -

I have found that playing cards, or classic board games, with teenagers and young adults is a wonderful way to laugh, and talk, and visit. One of my sons (in his 20's) was getting ready to go to work, but had about an hour of leisure before he had to leave. I brought out the word game - "Boggle," and we had the most wonderful time finding words using the three - minute "hourglass" timer. He left for work in a cheerful state of happiness, and with a love for home.

The Gardening -

Part of the day was spent in walking the property. I checked on my lilacs out front. They are beautiful and have such a wonderful scent! I picked some to put in a mason jar on my kitchen table. Then I walked out to the back grounds and checked on my blueberry bushes and strawberry garden. I saw that I needed to weed the garden, but because I am a known neglecter of plants, I did not do the work. I will get to it very soon, perhaps later today. Once I start the work, in the sunshine of the day, I know it will be a pleasant task.

The Laundry and the Cleaning -

I gathered up some clothes to wash. Then I did a little dusting and sweeping in the parlour. As the clothes went through the cycle of the machine, I straightened pillows, and did a little organizing. I hung up some of the wet clothes to dry, and then arranged my lilacs to look extra pretty on the kitchen table. The work of tidying and making things look pretty brought me a great deal of happiness.

Winding Down the Day -

The supper hour will always be a favorite time for me. It is when all are called to a pretty, set table to enjoy a home -cooked meal. We hear the prayer from father, thanking the Lord for the food, then we enjoy the nourishment and gentle conversation of pleasant things. As the sun sets, all the curtains and drapes are closed. Soon it is Bible time and the singing of hymns. We hear the Scripture read and take our turn reading. The we sing an old, classic song from the hymn book to warm the heart.

Another simple day has ended.

These are just the pleasant joys of family time and homemaking. We can all have these happy times with a great deal of peace, if we make the effort to do them, regardless of our circumstances. Are there moments of conflict? Is there a time of sadness or some worry? Then when peace is restored, get back to the simple tasks of making a home. We do the good things, in the middle of normal trials of life. This is what brings peace and happiness to our homes.

35
Financial Peace for 25 Cents

I have heard of Dave Ramsey and read some of his books. I know he has some kind of a radio program and helps many people manage their finances. I also attended a class on finances (through our church) many years ago, that was from his company. I love reading on the topic of careful use of money from a Biblical perspective.

Before Dave Ramsey, there was Larry Burkett. I found his books when I was a young mother in the late 1980's. I love anything he wrote, or taught, about managing money. I have his, *"The Complete Guide to Managing your Money,"* published in the 1980's. I have read it several times and love it. I plan to read it again this coming winter.

There is an incredible need for constant reminders and teachings on Biblical handling of our money. I am grateful for those who have made it their life work to help others have financial peace.

This month we attended our town's annual yard sale, which benefits our museum. I found a large box called, *"Financial Peace University"* with a price listed for a mere 25 cents. I did not blink. I did not flinch. I did not hesitate. I bought it immediately. It is the 2007 edition. It is missing a book: *"Financial Peace Revisited,"* but has most everything else, in almost - new condition. There are 16 audio CDs on subjects including: a spending plan; getting out of debt; emergency fund; insurance; giving; and retirement planning. Even though I already know about most of this, and have been practicing this type of living for most of my life, I will listen this coming winter while I do my sewing, crocheting, and kitchen work. It is always good to be reminded of that which is good!

There are many places we can acquire an education in financial peace for free, or for very little money. I have found Dave Ramsey books for free in a discard bin at our local library. I have seen other helpful books at our museum's annual yard sale. I prefer reading a real book, or watching a DVD on my television set, rather than being on the internet. There are many ways to be encouraged and motivated to manage our money in a way that brings glory to God, and gives us peace. This is the type of Biblical wisdom we need to keep passing on to the younger generation.

36
A Day of Homemaking

I have been trying to stay home as much as possible. It is so much easier to do projects, and cook and bake, when one is not rushed, or worn out, from errands. When I focus on staying home, things are slow -paced and peaceful.

I made homemade pizza this morning. I made several for the freezer and some for the grandchildren, in case they stopped by during the lunch hour. I had planned to make homemade wheat bread too, but didn't know if I could manage all the work. I have not been to the store in several days and we were running out of many things. I have not made wheat bread for quite some time, but I thought it would be a good kitchen project. By early afternoon it was time to start the bread.

Soon 4 of my sweet grand-babies arrived with their mother. They had been at a friend's house for lunch and were delighted to see me making bread dough. I had just started the batter. They were so excited to watch.

The children were, in fact, hungry. They watched me knead the dough (for 10 tiring minutes!) and put the dough aside for the first rising. I took some of the pizzas out of the freezer to make for the children.

The babies colored, told us stories, made us laugh, and were great helpers. They enjoyed their 2nd lunch and then it was time for them to get back home. We would see them again soon.

Throughout the day I worked on the dough and read about the Depression -era from a book called, "*When The Banks Closed We Opened our Hearts.*" This is an excellent book full of first- hand accounts of daily life with very little money. It is so inspiring!

I kept looking out the window to see the beautiful landscape out front. I wanted to take a walk around the property, but didn't seem to have time. There were two loaves of wheat bread baking in the oven. The scent was amazing!

I finally told my husband I wanted to take a quick walk. We checked the timer on the oven, found that we had exactly 8 minutes, and headed out to the back property. We visited the strawberry garden, the river, the blueberry bushes, and our cucumber garden. The afternoon sun was shining through the trees, glistening onto the green grass. It was such a beautiful day.

I rushed back indoors in plenty of time to get the bread out of the oven. After a short time of cooling, we were able to have a few pieces with butter. It was so good!

It is now late in the day and I have just a few little cleaning projects to do. I am trying to rest as much as possible. It is an ordeal to make food from scratch. But if those are the only major things I do in a day, I can manage. In just a little while, I will have a cup of tea and rest while watching "*Little House on the Prairie*," on DVD, for some old-time inspiration in simple living.

37
Writing Letters by the Lantern

We have an old-fashioned lantern. It uses lamp oil and a wick. We light it using a wooden match. We can make it bright, or dim, by using a little knob on the side. I thought it would be lovely and pleasant to sit by this lantern, at my parlour table, and write some letters.

I set up the area with a table cloth, the lantern, my notebook, and a pen. I had a stack of correspondence, in a little box, and was ready to get to work. In the background, was the gentle sound of old hymns playing on my kitchen radio. I started to write an old-fashioned letter.

The sun was going down, and the room got darker. I turned up the brightness on the lantern, but still struggled to see clearly. My vision is not as well as it was in my youth, but I was still enjoying the old-fashioned light.

By this time the sun had set. The only light was a gentle flickering from the lantern. I had to give up. It was time to turn on the modern lamp, by the couch. What a blessing to have a good, strong light to see well in the evening hours! I think I will just use the old lantern in the late afternoon hours, just to inspire a bit of nostalgia, a sense of simplicity, and an old-fashioned remembrance, of peaceful living.

38
Summer Heat in Rural Vermont

The summer heat has been very difficult this year. We live in the beautiful mountains of northern Vermont. But we still have some very warm days. It has frequently been in the 80's. I don't think I could handle living in Florida or in Texas where, I am told, the heat gets to be in the 90's and 100's. We recently had some missionaries come to speak at our church. They live in Texas and told us the work they are doing there. They briefly described the heat and told us it is much cooler here in Vermont! It gave me a grateful perspective.

To keep cool here at home, I close the blinds in certain rooms throughout the house. This blocks the heat of the sun. Our upstairs parlour has burgundy, sheer, curtains. The sun comes gently through this to give us natural light. But the strong heat of the sun is lessened. It also makes the room look extra peaceful and comfortable.

When we walk towards the river (bordering our back property), there is a coolness in the air that is refreshing. We also have many shade trees. But I can only take so much time outdoors during hot days.

I love having box - fans in our old windows. This brings much fresh, cool mountain air into our home. It keeps us comfortable.

It usually cools off in the evenings, or when there is an occasional rain. There is nothing like the beauty of rain glistening on the trees, and lush green landscape, here in Vermont. The beauty keeps us grateful.

I know that our bitterly cold winters will arrive very quickly. We start preparing for the cold season in spring, and work diligently throughout the summer months. *"The Old Farmer's Almanac"* tells us our first frost date is in September. There is often a bit of a chill as early as August, here in the northeast. This is why I am enjoying the hot summer days as much as I can!

39
The Anniversary of a Family

Every year, on our wedding anniversary, I try to do something to make the day special. I want it to be different than all the other ordinary days. We live very simply, and do not have much money to spend, so it takes extra effort to be creative.

As my children have all grown up, and we became grandparents, I started to realize that a wedding anniversary is not just about the husband and wife. It is about the legacy of the entire family. It is a celebration of the family unit.

I have a tiny book called, "*Wedding Memories*" that my husband's grandmother gave to us after we were married. It has pictures of the simple ceremony. I have carried it with us through the years, through all the moves, through every trial, through sickness and health, and through the happy times. I place this on the table each year to look through, and to remember.

About seven years ago, just before our first grandchild was born, I created a binder for pictures. I gave it a title: "*The History of Mr. and Mrs. White and their decedents.*" The cover has a faded picture of my husband and I on our wedding day. It has now been 31 years since we got married. Our marriage has been blessed with five children and nine grandchildren.

Each year, I gather up a few pictures to add to this binder of family memories. I realized today, as I was setting the table with a white tablecloth, some pretty fake flowers, a lovely candle, and my books of memories, that this is not just about a wedding. It is about maintaining and working hard, to keep the family strong.

The family is something of great value. It is something that requires a great deal of humility and of gratefulness. We need to keep working on cheering each other up, encouraging one another, and being there when we are needed. We need to value the family. We need to keep building up the home and strengthening our relationships.

How easily each one of us could fall! How easily an argument, or holding a grudge, could destroy the family! Life is too short. We need to be on guard and always learning to be peacemakers. My Mother used to say, "There but by the grace of God, go I." God's mercy and long-suffering towards us, and the blessing He gives us, is what keeps us going each day.

There are good and bad days for all of us in this life. But remember to celebrate, and focus on, the good and happy times. An anniversary of the family is a wonderful day to look at old pictures, and remember our parents and grandparents, as well as our children and grandchildren. This helps bring security, as we link the generations, and see that our lives are about more than just today.

The Christian home, with the Bible as the foundation of all we do, is an incredible blessing to all, in every generation. A wedding anniversary is a good day to look back at all the times of answered prayer, of blessings, of beautiful memories, and recommit ourselves to trusting the Lord, and of giving Him all our burdens. This is what will bring us great peace and joy.

40
The Four Little Tasks of Home

It is nice to have a set routine of work to do at home. One can go about the day with a remembrance of certain housekeeping duties that are necessary for each day. Then, during the many breaks for rest (or visiting with guests, or a pleasant talk on the telephone), one finds refreshment and courage to go on. The times of work, and the times of rest, done with quiet courage, provide happiness in our homemaking.

The Four Little Tasks of Home

1. There is the breakfast hour, which includes tea-time. First, we prepare the meal and set a table. I often set up a tray- table and sit in the parlour before anyone else is awake. I am an early riser, so I have my tea while the sun is just beginning to rise. I enjoy this quiet time of resting from the brief bit of morning work.

   Later, when the family has their eggs and toast, or fresh baked muffins with fruit, it is time to do the dishes. We wash the table and the counters and do the sweeping. All the work of tidying, and making things neat, are part of the breakfast duties.

2. Often, during the morning hours, we do the laundry or the dusting and vacuuming. Each day has its special work. It may be Wednesday is for washing floors. Perhaps Thursday is for cleaning the bathroom? The mid-morning hours are a good time, for many of us, to do these special duties of making a home look pretty.

3. The Lunch hour is such a wonderful time to stop and rest. We put out a fresh, clean tablecloth. I love my white-and-teal checkered cloth. It looks so homey and old fashioned. We can set up our plates and napkins. We can do this, even if we are just serving grilled cheese sandwiches, pickles, and chips! It makes the lunch - work like a reward, when we sit at that pretty table, and rest, and eat, while we enjoy the family. Next, we do the sweeping and the dishes, much like we did in the morning.

4. The dinner hour is such a precious time in the day. I often start working on the evening meal at 3 in the afternoon. I work slowly and take lots of breaks. Sometimes I peel potatoes and start getting a little casserole ready to bake. Other times I might do much of the work for a pan of lasagna. I like to put these pans of prepared food in the refrigerator, and then just take them out to bake, when it is just about dinner time. That way, I get a great deal of rest between all the work.

Sitting with the family, and hearing the blessing (or the prayer before the meal), is such a peaceful experience. It is lovely to just sit and enjoy dinner at the end of a long day. Then the work of tidying, doing the dishes, and sweeping the floor happens. We make everything look neat and pretty. But I do not like to rush. I do not want to just "get the work over-with." I take my time and go at a steady pace. The work of cleaning, and accomplishing the beautiful work of making a neat home, makes me happy. It also brings peace.

These four tasks of homemaking do not take a great deal of effort. They may seem simple and ordinary. They may seem mundane. But if we dress up in something pretty, wearing an apron, and keeping our hair up in a pretty style, we may find ourselves enjoying the work. I have an old blue-and-white gingham apron that I love to wear. It is getting old and ragged. I will have to make a new one this coming fall. I need a fresh supply of lovely aprons to wear as I do the housekeeping.

When we look extra nice as we do our work, we can find joy in the labor. Doing the little tasks of keeping house, each day, with a feeling of contentment, will bring a true feeling of comfort and happiness to the family. It will help them feel welcome and loved, in a happy and simple home.

41
Evening Devotions

I love the end of the day, when the family can gather all around and have evening prayers. This can be such a special time of reading the Bible, singing some hymns, and then having a time of prayer.

Our routines will often change as the family grows, or when schedules fluctuate. When the children are little, it is more common that all are home at the same time. As they get older, they may have evening classes or work obligations. Sometimes Dad may be working a night shift, and the family Bible time is better organized earlier in the day. We will often change the routine as needed. But there is nothing like closing out the day with a simple time of Evening Devotions.

How very precious is a habit of evening devotions! If they are generally done at the same time each day, such as at 7 p.m., it produces a stability of a beautiful tradition. No matter who is available at home to participate, it could become a regular routine.

This time of family worship could be just Mother, or many in the family together, depending on who is at home. It could be a time to read a verse in the Bible and sing one hymn. Or it could be a reading of several passages of Scripture and a few songs to sing. It may only be a simple time of precious prayer, at the same hour each evening, day after day, week after week, year after year.

Whether it be a brief time of quiet worship, or a longer time, it is such a precious spiritual habit, that will close out the day with gratefulness and praise to our dear Lord. When Dad is away from home, or older children are away at that hour, they can know that Mother is at home praying for them, during the evening devotions. This will comfort and soothe weary hearts, and help give them spiritual courage.

This is a beautiful way to end each day.

42
One Must Not Complain

I found myself making comments, during general kitchen chatter, about being tired or in pain. I would be washing dishes and saying hello to one of the grown children as they walked by. I would say simple things like, "I am so tired today." Then, I would smile and have little chats with the family. But my comments of, "my back hurts this morning," or "This is making me tired," were becoming as normal as discussing the weather. It had become a habit to murmur, fret, and complain, with a sweet smile. This was not necessary. It was a problem.

That old saying, "If you can't say something nice, don't say anything at all," comes to mind. I suddenly realized that my words were not nice. They did not bring cheer to others. They did not brighten the day for us all. I could have just as easily kept those murmuring comments to myself and instead said, "How are you? Isn't it a pretty day this morning?" Or even, "I will sit and have tea with you as soon as I finish the sweeping." This gave me things to look forward to, instead of drawing attention to, and dwelling on, the negative things we all go through.

We are all tired. We all have times of pain. How very precious would it be if I kept quiet until I thought of something sweet and uplifting to say? This little habit of complaining, in normal conversation, changed very quickly. It became fun to think of something nice to say. I enjoyed seeing happier faces around me, rather than ones of concern and worry. I had learned it is better to cheer others along, than to dwell on one's own suffering.

43
Passing the Time in the Kitchen

It can be very overwhelming to do a great deal of kitchen work unless one is happy. I like to have a cheerful kitchen. The cabinets are painted a light purple color. The walls are a delicate pastel green. I have ruffled curtains on the window and a pretty view, out back, while I wash dishes.

But the best item in my entire kitchen is the CD player. Here is what helps me delight in my work. I listen to old time gospel sermons when I am making pizza or bread dough. If I will be in the room for a long time, a good sermon helps me pass the time.

I make brownies, cookies, and cinnamon cake, while listening to soothing hymns. I do the dishes, and sweep the floor, as the sound of old, country gospel comes through my kitchen radio.

I never understood how people could stand for such long periods of time to work in the kitchen. I have two stools and a large butcher-block counter. I sit when I wash the dishes. I sit when I make up batters and doughs. I get to rest as I work, so I can endure the labor in a joyful way.

There is nothing quite so spiritually nourishing as listening to old sermons and hymns, while passing the time in the kitchen.

44
Don't Forget the Bell

I have a little dinner bell I keep on the parlour hutch. It is something I often use at our tea time, to add a little bit of fun and formality to the experience. When our grown children and grandchildren are here, I love to ring the bell as a reminder that we are just about to have a treat, or a meal. At times, I get too busy and forget all about my fun routines.

The other day, some of the grandchildren were sitting at the lunch table. I heard a sweet voice from my 3-year-old grandson. He has the most charming, little voice. As we all sat down together, he looked at me and said, "Me`me, don't forget to ring the bell." I could not help but smile.

I jumped right up and went over to the hutch. I rang the bell a few times, just for fun. All the children turned to see. "It is time to eat." I announced. The children were delighted.

45
Keeping a Frugal Kitchen

I have been helping others, in our extended family, for the past few months. Funds in each of our homes have been severely limited. We have had to be very careful with our kitchen shopping. While I do not believe in keeping a scarce and empty pantry, it is difficult to keep a stocked pantry on a reduced income.

I like to keep plenty of flour, baking powder, eggs, butter, and sugar on hand. I can bake cinnamon cake, muffins, and cookies. These homemade treats help keep us full, and are more nourishing than store-bought snacks. I am also careful to offer fresh produce, especially carrots and apples, on a daily basis. We have some canned and frozen food, when fresh is not possible. We must keep ourselves nourished in an economical way.

I have had some of the grown children visit recently, and look into the cabinets and refrigerator, with a mention that we did not have much to eat. This was because they may have been used to some convenience food items, such as frozen pizza and other quick dinner foods, that are popular and enjoyable to the younger generation.

These were never in my own childhood home. My mother never bought such things. These types of food are very expensive, and do not provide as much wholesome, nutrition as homemade items. So, while the grown children may have not seen much in my kitchen, I had enough resources to bake, and cook, and produce nourishing meals, until more funds were available to replenish the limited pantry.

We have been sharing ideas, among our households, of what to cook and bake using what is on hand, and with what is affordable. Sometimes we will go to each other's houses to share a treat, or a meal, when times are tough. We are always welcoming and hospitable, as if we all share in each other's bounty and homes.

Often, I will package up some fresh baked goods to send home to the grandchildren. They do not leave here without a snack, such as cookies, brownies, or some muffins that have just been baked.

Baking food from scratch takes a great deal of effort, but is essential when one must keep a frugal kitchen.

Sometimes we talk about the food we have enjoyed, in the past, from our favorite restaurants. These were always a rare treat. I also think of steak dinners and other expensive meals that are often served in wealthy restaurants. That type of food is not commonly served in humble households. When one is used to plain, homemade, economical food, one loses a taste for wealthier meals.

We are content with simple food and mother's baked treats. This is home - cooked food that has been known for generations by practical housewives. It also makes us incredibly grateful for a true Thanksgiving feast each November. We also dearly appreciate a birthday cake, and holiday treats, at each season. We appreciate these times much more because we are not indulging, and overspending, in everyday life.

In traditional Jewish homes, special food was always purchased for the blessed, weekly Sabbath. This was the great day of rest, and gratefulness; to focus on the Lord and our incredible blessings! We may have plain food, and do plain labor, each day of the week, but the Sabbath was reserved for special food, much like old time families offered a large Sunday dinner after church. These are precious times of enjoying special food that one had to carefully scrimp and save, to obtain.

A frugal kitchen is a great lesson in hard work and contentment. It helps prevent a great deal of waste, of food and money. It also avoids excess, in overly rich and expensive food, since we choose the more humble, budget friendly, version of meals. One can build up a savings, from the grocery money, if one learns to be simple in taste, and careful in spending.

46
Paper Napkins for Grand-girl

I keep a little box on the hutch in our parlour. It is full of a variety of napkins. There are handmade, and store-bought ones, along with several made of paper. Whenever some of the grandchildren are here to eat, I will ask 6-year-old grand-girl for help. She might be reading a book, playing with toys, or putting away her coloring supplies. I will say, "Will you get the napkins for everyone?" She gets right to work with a nod. She always looks so sweet, as she lingers by the hutch, selecting the napkins she wants to use. Then she walks slowly around the table, placing a napkin at each place-setting. We do this every single time we have snack, or a meal, here at Grandmother's house.

One day, just as the children were getting ready to go back to their own home, grand-girl asked me if she could take some napkins home with her. "Of course," I smiled, and encouraged her sweet request. I helped her gather several napkins, some white, some with a decoration of spring flowers. We folded them up and placed them in her little bag.

Did I ever tell you about her little bag? Every time she visits me, she has a purse, or toy tote bag, that she fills up with things from home. There is always some little toy inside, or her favorite stuffed puppy. It was in this bag that we placed the napkins for her to keep.

A few days later, the mother of these dear grandbabies told me how very happy her little girl was at meal time. She would take out some napkins, from her bag, and slowly walk around the table at her own house. Each member of the family received a napkin from grandmother's house. It was reported to me that she did this at every meal. "Her supply is almost gone." I was told after some days.

Very soon, I will have to offer another stack of paper napkins for grand-girl to take home. She is such a precious little homemaker. She loves to keep her family comfortable and happy, with the dear little manners, of keeping a nice napkin at table.

47
Heritage of Family Bibles

My father was often seen reading his Bible. He would be in the recliner, with a nearby lamp to brighten the text as he read. I would also see him sitting at a desk, as he studied the Scriptures. I will always remember that about him. When we children were young, he gave each of us a Bible of our own, with our name inscribed on the cover. It is a cherished possession that I still have, all these many years later.

When my own five children were little, they were each given Bibles once they were old enough to read. I would gather them around me, after saying, "go get your Bibles." Each had their own, and took turns reading. We also had hymn books to sing from. This was daily worship, or family Bible time. It was a little church in our home.

Now that I am a grandmother of eleven, I have the same opportunity to share my love of the old family Bible. The babies see our Bibles here at home. They want to take down a copy and settle on the couch to read. A couple of years ago, when one of the boys started Kindergarten, he wanted to borrow my Bible. I said it was time for me to order one for him, to keep for his own. A few weeks later, when it arrived in the mail, he was so happy and thankful. It is a traditional, black Bible. He reads it each day and loves it.

Last year, one of the grand - girls entered Kindergarten. Some weeks ago, she asked me something like, "Do you remember when you gave a Bible to my brother?" I knew she wanted her own copy. I love these precious opportunities to share something that I cherish. I like to wait until they show an interest. I want to know they are ready. I quickly ordered a pink one this time. It is a "gift and award," KJV Bible, from Hendrickson publishers. (They cost about $5 each.)

I handed this very, special book to my little grand-girl. She is a new reader and will take her time with the words inside. I showed her the index and how to find the page where the Psalms could be found. We turned the pages to Psalm 117. I told her it was a special chapter that her Mother used to read to me all the time. Then I wanted to save the page for her, but the Bible does not have a ribbon book marker.

Grand-girl and I took a quick look inside my sewing box. We found a little package of white lace, hem material. We cut out a couple of pieces. I told her, "These will be your book marks. You can keep one on the page for Psalm 117. The other book mark is for any special page you want." She was so happy and proud of her new treasure.

The other day, the Mother of these dear children told me that they sit and read their Bibles together. These are the same, sweet grandbabies that have gone to church with me a few times, when they were younger. I would give them tiny, baby Bibles of blue and pink; One for each child to hold as we sat in the pew of church. I remember them being so sweet and respectful. They were so well behaved, at having the privilege of getting all dressed up, and going to church with grandmother.

There is a beautiful Christian heritage of owning Bibles in the home. This legacy of reading, and cherishing the Word of God, is such a blessing to the family. It is something little ones should remember about Mother and Dad. They should remember this about Grandmother and Grandfather. The love of the Bible ought to be passed on throughout the generations. This can be done by example, and by just catching that sweet spirit, of seeing such joy and peace, in reading the old family Bible.

48
Supplies for the Household

In old books, I often read of housewives (in the 1800's) who had to hand-sew the family clothing. They would stay up late in the twilight hours, after all the day's work was completed, to do the sewing and the mending. Perhaps little Betsy needed a few warm dresses for the fall season. Maybe Papa needed some shirts for work. Then little Philip had to have a pair of overalls, because his old ones were all worn out. This was the constant type of work, that Mother had to do, to supply the many needs of her family.

I don't think it ever entered her mind to sell her creations. Like many dear Mothers of old time, she was not seeking financial gain. Her only thought was the work she could reasonably do, to take care of her home. I am sure she must have made tablecloths, cloth napkins, pillowcases, and curtains. Perhaps she made little ruffles to trim the curtains. Maybe she embroidered handkerchiefs to bring skill and beauty to her possessions. Her handmade quilts, and afghans, were made to keep the family warm and happy.

While she did all this work, without pay, she must have prayed for her family. She must have talked to the Lord, in quiet prayers, about their daily needs and troubles. She thought of Philip as she made his overalls. He was a dear boy, wasn't he? Oh, how she loved him! She thanked the Lord for Betsy's cheerful personality as she made dresses in colors that would delight her little girl. As she made Papa's shirts, she did them with great care. He would be so thankful for all the extra care she put into his clothing, knowing she was a good and prudent wife. Surely, she was a gift from the Lord. As she sewed, she prayed for his job, and thanked her Heavenly Father for this good man, who worked so hard to provide for his family.

Mother made a steady supply of dust rags out of worn-out clothing. She made patches for Philip's clothes, and she made many beautiful napkins out of leftover scraps of material. She truly was a virtuous wife, and mother, who thought of her own home, as she supplied for all the needs of her own household. No thought of riches or worldly gain entered her mind. Her life, and her focus, were on the precious family she felt so blessed to have. This was an old-fashioned home, with an ordinary life, where Mother lived on the income the Lord, Himself, provided for her. She had no need of fret, or worry, as she did her hand-sewing, each evening, by the hearth. Her quiet, peaceful life, as she did the old familiar duties, was such a joy to behold. It was like a candle in the window, guiding others to the old paths. Many watched her (from afar) tending her little home, and craved such a simple life, of faith and trust in the dear Lord.

49
An Evening Walk in the Garden

It had been a restful weekend. The weather was lovely, with just a bit of gentle wind blowing the leaves in the sunlight. I had made homemade pizza for lunch and was trying to get a good afternoon rest. By early evening, I remembered that Papa had offered to walk in the garden with me. I got a big bowl to gather a small harvest. As I stepped on the last stair leading to the downstairs living room, he got right up, as he noticed I was ready for our outing.

We walked slowly out the door, enjoying the beauty of an early evening. "Should we check the lettuce first?" He asked me. I followed him to our small plants. "Which ones would you like?" I nodded and sweetly suggested, "Whichever ones you think are ready." He always picks out four good leaves for my little salads. It was another short walk to the larger, homemade garden. We were surrounded by a variety of greenery, trees, and wildflowers at the edge of our property. We could hear the river (bordering our Estate), rushing along, and an occasional sound of wildlife enjoying the day.

We looked at all the tomatoes that were coming in. These are all for Papa, since I dislike this type of produce. I loved to see all the new growth and how well it was thriving. I am happy for him and say, "Look at how many tomatoes you will have!"

We soon found a few peapods for me. He picked three or four and placed them in my bowl. "Is there a cucumber ready for me today?" I inquired. He looked through the vines and discovered one that was ready for today. He always cleans up whatever produce is ready (like a gentleman) before he places it in my bowl.

I held my bowl as we walked away from the garden. What a blessing to have fresh food from one's own home! We walked along the grounds to see the sights, visit our strawberry garden, and see if any of my miniature roses, out front by the porch, were in bloom.

The sun was slowly lingering, in its downward path, as the day was winding down. We walked quietly and gratefully into the house. We would walk again tomorrow.

50
Poor in Spirit

There is a passage of Scripture we commonly call, "The Beatitudes." It begins with the beautiful words of, "Blessed are the poor in spirit; for theirs is the kingdom of heaven." I have read this many times throughout my life. It is from Matthew chapter 5. The Beatitudes are all so beautiful and comforting to read, and to recite.

I was with a very dear lady, sitting at her kitchen table. She was reading that passage and suddenly said, "What does 'poor in spirit' mean?" I had not thought to analyze it, I had simply loved it. So many times, we read the Bible and get little glimpses of joy to feed and nourish us, but we may not always stop to meditate, or slowly sup, on the preciousness of Scripture.

Back at home, a few days later, we were thinking about the joy of prayer, and the holiness of speaking to the Lord with quiet prayers and thanksgiving. I realized that prayer and being "poor in spirit" had a great deal to do with one another.

I looked through my pulpit commentaries. This incredible set of books was once owned by my own father. He was the son of a revival preacher. He, himself, as a young man, was a street preacher. He spent his life studying the Bible and was dedicated to the Lord.

I found great encouragement in the description of "poor in spirit" in the pages of the preacher's commentary. It described a lowliness of self. It described a person with no worldly ambition. I thought of a person who was not puffed up or full of self. It was a poverty of self.

There are some who put others above themselves. They live a life of graceful service to others. They do this without seeking reward. They have an incredible closeness to the Lord that gives them such a sweet and gentle spirit. The closer they get to the Lord, the less of "self" or "selfishness" is evident. These are the kindest and most gentle-natured people we can know. They are the Lord's dear workers and are greatly needed in this corrupt world.

To ascend to this wonderful and blessed state, in this life, is to love prayer. This is a state of almost constant communion with God. It is a time of asking for guidance, wisdom, and a calling for help in all things. As one thanks the Lord for every moment, every blessing, one becomes content and grateful. One forms such a bond with the Lord, that the ties of this earthly life loosen, to the point that only living for God is the blessed fruit, and joy, of one's life. This, to me, is to be "poor in spirit."

51
Little Walks in the Garden

I try to take a walk on our property each afternoon. I love to check on the wildflowers and look at all the trees. We have two strawberry plots, some blueberries, and other little gardens scattered throughout the grounds. There are many birds, whose sweet singing is such a joy to hear. We have noticed a mother and baby deer have settled themselves in the woods at the edge of our property. I have seen them a few times walking across the front yard. My husband, who is often on the back grounds, has captured them on video and camera, as he goes about his work in the garage and garden.

Most days, I have noticed my miniature roses, out front, have new buds developing. I get excited, each time I visit them, hoping they have blossomed. Somehow, when they are just about to open up, I notice they have completely disappeared. I wonder if, in the quiet of the dawn, mother deer snatches my beautiful flowers away. It makes me smile, thinking about it, each time one goes missing.

On some of my walks about the land, my husband will drive over to me on his riding mower and ask if I would like a ride. He takes me all over the property and it is such a fun part of our summer days. Soon the leaves will change colors and then scatter over the lush, green grass. Winter comes early in northern Vermont. That will be the end of our walks and of our working outdoors.

I cherish these peaceful walks in the gardens. I love the beauty around me. Nothing else matters on these little journeys throughout our days. We only think of family, and home, and of a gratefulness to God for every moment He has given to us.

52
Enough Money to be Content

It used to be common for families to live content on whatever income they were earning. These were families who lived humble lives focusing on living for the Lord and not for themselves. There was no such thing as pocket money, to spend on a whim or for personal amusement. Families needed to pay for food, shelter, clothing, and the occasional treat that brought a bit of joy and happiness to their days.

I cannot imagine what it would be like to use money for the purpose of simply passing the time of day. Life, and living, does not revolve around the spending of cash or of getting into debt to acquire things one cannot afford. This modern way of thinking, brought to us by years of easy credit and advertising, has caused a great deal of confusion on how to live simply on limited means.

People have gotten into a form of slavery to debt payments. This takes away necessary money and resources they could have used on precious efforts of benevolence to those around them. It is a joy to give and to help others! Such happiness cannot come from just using money for ourselves.

To have enough to pay the bills and to feed the family is good and noble. To provide an old-fashioned life, avoiding debt and overindulgence, brings a great deal of peace and contentment. It also brings freedom.

53
Old Time Homemaking

Last week, in the early hours of the morning, we had to drive through a nearby town. The roads were quiet and peaceful without much traffic. As we were enjoying the scenery, an unusual sight appeared. It was a beautiful horse and buggy coming down the road. An Amish family were sitting comfortably in four of the seats, heading home from an early morning drive. This is a rare vision, for us, because a few Amish families only moved here a few years ago. I am always inspired by their quiet, old fashioned way of living. It was like watching a living museum as we passed by them. I wanted some of their peace, knowing they never watch the news or hear it on the radio. They continue on each day living their daily, precious ways that many of us have lost sight of. It is a way of being in the world, but not of it. It is great trust and faith in the Lord for all things.

This has encouraged me in my homemaking. The last few weeks, I have been home a great deal. I am avoiding the stores as much as possible. I have plenty of time to pace myself throughout the day. I clean, and cook, and rest. It is a blessing to be productive at home, doing the old time work that housewives have always done, throughout the generations.

We have had to set up a garden this year. The seeds were ordered in the beginning of April. Our last frost, in our region, is in late May. We have been enjoying wonderful, homegrown food. Even though we do not have much money, I have been able to go outside, each day, and gather a modest harvest to have a simple lunch.

It is easier to live on a small income, when one must rely on Yankee ingenuity to get by with limited resources. Even though we have a great deal to learn about growing our own food, and getting the energy to do the work, we have been able to enjoy fresh food from our own property.

My husband has been gathering whatever scrap supplies he could find, from our garage, to build a humble garden this season. (His disability causes him to work much slower than he would like. He has to take many breaks.) We are growing peas, tomatoes, lettuce, cucumbers, strawberries, and blueberries. We hope to add more next year.

I love to take a break from my housework to go outside and walk the grounds. We found some wild blackberries at the perimeter of the property. It was such a sweet treat on a hot summer day. As we walk, we check the plants, our flowers, linger at the river behind our humble Estate, and then stop to do some necessary weeding of the garden. We walk and work together so the burden does not rest too heavily on one person.

Sometimes, in the late afternoon, I go into one of the front rooms. I have rearranged furniture and set up a card table in this room. I like to listen to an old record of gospel music, sit at the table, enjoying the view, and do a little writing. Some days I will simply sit by the French doors and do some hand-sewing. This is an incredible room, to just think on that which is lovely, and feel the blessing of peace, and joy, knowing the Lord will take care of us.

I have been listening to "The Isom Lee Trio." This was a church singing group of a father and his two adult daughters. Mr. Lee was a preacher who encouraged and inspired whoever was blessed to hear his sermons. Many years ago, my father gave me a tape of Reverend's Lee's last sermon. It is incredible and such a blessing. Now I have a record of their old-time gospel singing. The songs and piano are something like you would hear in old southern churches. It is from another time, a precious time, of faith and godly living that we dearly need in these modern days.

Dad had a record player here, when he and mother used to live with us. They lived here with us for 9 years. At one point we had four generations living together in this old house. I now keep his record player in our front room. While I sit and hand sew cloth napkins, or do some mending, I can listen to the hymns of Tennessee Ernie Ford or the Isom Lee Trio on the old record player.

Listening to the gospel songs, from the old days, encourages me in living the old ways. This was a time when family was the center of home life, rather than materialism or the constant pursuit of entertainment. It was a time when money was used for practical purposes. Frivolity was rare.

Here at our Vermont Estate, we live simply and on my husband's income. We are a one - income family. I am a housewife and am grateful for the privilege of staying home. But there is a cost. There is a great deal of old-time work to live within one's humble means. We must think of duty and practicality. There is plenty of work we must do, each day, even if we struggle with our health.

We are very careful with the funds we are provided with. We have to find ways to save money for emergencies, annual bills, and repairs. One of my children called it a "Walton's Budget," referring to "*The Waltons*" television program. The family saved up to meet the needs of **problems** and **necessities**. They always expected many rainy days and had to save all they could. I love that thought of calling it a "Walton's Budget." These modern days, people save for vacations, to buy a new boat, or to go on a shopping spree. Many have no idea how to live on a limited income. It is old time family homemaking. It is a way of life that brings great peace and rest, in simple living, with a great faith in God.

Autumn

{Photograph on Previous Page: The countryside, near Mrs. White's home.}

54
Days of Housekeeping

I remember the early years of my marriage. We had moved into our first home. It was completely empty. We had limited furniture and not many possessions. The boxes were few. We had packages of brand-new items from our wedding. Soon we had to find curtains and bedding and a kitchen table. My parents had given us a couch, a bureau, and a few other pieces of furniture. We had to set up housekeeping with limited means. Because we did not have much, it was easier to keep things neat and clean.

These days, many of us are fighting clutter and an abundance of items. The common teaching out there is to "purge" and "declutter." This is because, over the years, we tend to accumulate more things than we seem to know what to do with. But we do not have to throw out things that are useful. We do not have to give away, or trash items, that we can neatly pack away for the future.

We often read of grandmother's attic and the old trunk full of treasures. This is where grandchildren come along and find wonderful things from the family's history. Often, an old shawl, toy truck, or precious book, finds a new home with one of the decedents. Sometimes, baby clothes are carefully stored away, because we should always expect a baby will, someday, enter our home again. I don't think any of these possessions should be purged. But we do have to get rid of junk and trash in order to have a neat home.

It can be quite an ordeal to keep a nice home when there is too much clutter around. Often, it is almost impossible to find enough energy to do the daily work, and take care of the family, while organizing our possessions at the same time. This is where having set days for specific housekeeping is helpful.

If we simplify the work into a weekday schedule, it may help keep us peaceful and happier. This work is over- and- above the normal tasks of preparing meals, making beds, taking care of the family, etc.

Expect to spend between 2 and 4 hours on each of these days. You might want to do a few hours in the morning, and then work again in the early afternoon. Take lots of breaks so that you are well rested. Get help from the family, if you still have children at home. Small children love to help with the work. Older children are often willing to help, if we are cheerful and offer to play board games, etc. during breaks. This makes the work a social event, and is more enjoyable.

Here is an example:

Monday -
Organize and Declutter. This work will always be necessary. It would be nice if it was part of our weekly routine. We may want to file papers, sort photographs, handle the bills and finances, pack up seasonal clothing, put away books, organize the closets, etc.

Tuesday-

Laundry, sewing, mending clothes, ironing, tidy drawers and closets, wash bedding.

Wednesday-

Do all the deep cleaning (bathrooms, wash floors, dust, vacuum, etc.) In my teenage years, working as a maid, it took us 2 hours to do the basics of deep cleaning for an entire house.

Thursday-

Grocery shopping and errands. I always get extra tired on days I have to go out. This is a good day to serve easy meals to keep things simple. Buying the groceries, using a carefully prepared shopping list, setting up the week's menus, and bringing it all home takes a great deal of frugal effort. (You might want to use this day to post next week's menu in the kitchen so you have your plans all ready in place.) Sometimes on these errands we may also have to stop at the bank, go to the library, or visit a relative.

Friday-

Heavy Baking and Cooking. This is a good day to bake a cake for the weekend. We might want to make easy food for next week's lunches to put in the freezer (like homemade pizza and lasagna).

    I believe one of the biggest obstacles of keeping a nice house is being overwhelmed by clutter and messes. Sometimes we end up throwing out things we really wanted to keep. We might do this because it is hard to keep home neat, and we often feel guilty for having so much stuff. It doesn't have to be this way. I believe that a good schedule of keeping set days to do certain work, including a day just for organizing, will make our homes more pleasant and easier to manage.

55
Sewing in the Guest Room

I have been worn out the last few days. The combination of stress (from worries) and taking care of the home and family gets to be too much for all of us at times. I spent much of the morning resting and doing little tasks of home-keeping.

I have also been watching *"Father Knows Best"* on DVD when I am too tired to do anything else. After a little break, I decided to get started on a little sewing project. I am making a set of six, hand-sewn cloth napkins. The fabric is already cut. I just need to iron the hems so I can pin them for sewing.

Papa helped me set up my ironing board. I soon realized I was too tired to stand up, so the board is right beside the bed in our guest room. I am amazed to find that it is the perfect solution to my problem. I can now just sit on the edge of the bed and iron. The board is at desk- level compared to the bed, so it is wonderful.

Since there are no current guests occupying this room, I will leave my sewing project on the ironing board, near the comfortable bed, and work at my leisure, here a little – and there a little, throughout the day. It will not be long before the pretty cloth napkins are ready. Then I can get started on a new apron.

56
At Grandmother's House

Some of the grandchildren spent the entire day here with me. Their Mother's car was in a repair shop, and we were waiting for the call to say it was all ready. We started by going in the Day room on our first floor. We have an old-fashioned television set where we can watch cute DVDs such as *"The Tangerine Bear."* I tell the children it is the Christmas bear movie. They always sit for a short time and then run off into the next room to play.

As the younger boys (ages 2 and 3) are building with blocks or piling up puzzle pieces into a tower, little 4-year-old grand-girl will suddenly notice that I am sitting quietly on the couch crocheting. We must always have a blanket, so she gets one for us and we share it. Next, she takes the ball of yarn and starts doing the routine work of loosening it, and setting up a pile of yarn, on the couch beside us, for me to work with. I will hear her say little comments as she works, "Oh this is too many. You don't need that much." And she will wrap some of it back onto the ball. Or she will say, "You need more. I will get you some." And she will unravel it again.

Once she ventured to say, "How do you do it, Me`me?" So, I showed her, ever so slowly, how to place the hook into a nearby loop. I even let her try it a few times. This delighted her so much, that when I had to leave the room for a few moments, Papa came looking for me to say, "Does she know how to Crochet?" I smiled knowing that she was probably trying to do it herself.

I quietly went back to the doorway to see the most sweetest sight, of her holding the finished work in one hand, and the crochet hook in the other, as she carefully wound it into little loop, after little loop. She looked up at me and smiled.

"Should we do the laundry now?" I asked her. "Or would you rather stay here and play with the boys?" She put down the yarn and bounded towards me, responding with "do the laundry!"

Her Mother was busy about the house, and checking on babies, while grand-girl and I went to do some chores. I took bits of wet clothing, out of the washing machine, and handed them down to her waiting hands. She piled the dryer with each bundle. Soon, that work was finished.

It was time for prayers and a snack. All the children were at the table having juice and homemade muffins. I had my tea. I needed to start another chore. Grand-girl looked at me, and warned, "Don't do the dishes without me."

It was not long before she was up and getting two kitchen stools. The wobbly one is for Me`me and the sturdy one is for grand-girl (so she doesn't fall). We sit side-by-side and do the work together as slowly as we like. There is never any rush to do the housekeeping.

The boys were now busy with play-dough and crayons at the kitchen table. Mother had to go out to the private school to pick up the oldest grand-boy. (He is six years old.) Her car was not yet ready, so one of the Uncles gave her a ride.

It was not long before there were 4 grandchildren here to brighten up the house with their wonderful noise, occasional outbursts, and happy laughter. It was time to make an early supper.

While mother did the cooking, grand-girl and I brought the clean clothes into my bedroom so we could fold it all. There was not much, so I gave her the large checkered tablecloth. She enjoys a challenge. While she worked with it on my carpeted floor, I visited with her Mother, and folded all the rest of the laundry and put it away. I told her that, "this little girl is a hard worker. She will need to rest."

I took all the children back downstairs to the day room and turned on a pleasant movie for them. I got a pillow and small blanket for each to lie down on the floor. Then I closed the curtains to bring a little quiet and dimness to the room. The children needed the ambiance of rest and quiet for just a little while, as their supper was being prepared upstairs. I knew they would not stop running, playing, and inventing their fun, if I did not gently settle them down for a quiet break. We all need times of rest.

After the children had their supper, their car was all ready. On went their coats, boots, and hats. Hugs, kisses, and goodbyes went all around the room. The children followed their mother eagerly out the door to head back to their own home. It has been a wonderful day at Grandmother's house.

57
Domestic Happiness

This year has been very difficult for my family, as well as for many others. There have been deaths in our extended family, and the missing of those close ones who have been in Heaven some years. We all have trials and hardships we have to go through.

Sometimes stress from extended family, personal loss, or the worries and burdens we feel about family members, as they struggle in life, can make us miserable. It is hard enough dealing with our own personal problems (such as chronic illness or paying bills), we have to learn not to take on the pain of those around us. We will always care. We will always worry. But we cannot let burdens take away our joy.

My husband has watched the movie "*Fireproof*" a couple of times this year, without me knowing. It gave him some good ideas and he has been extra kind. I have learned from him how important it is to be good and pleasant and to give to those we love, without conditions, or expecting anything. It is a kindness based on personal contentment in the Lord. This is part of being happy.

Some of us have grown children who are going through painful trials. This hurts our mother hearts. It can overwhelm us with grief and cause us to always try to "help" or "fix it" for them. But we have to learn to give the burden, and the worry, where it belongs, in the Hands of God through prayer! He cares for the sparrows, takes care of His children, and He will surely take care of these trials.

There is a hymn that has been going through my mind over the last evening. It was a lesson to me on how to be happy, reminding me that burdens should be left at the foot of the cross, and I can walk away in peace and happiness. The song is "*At the Cross*" by Isaac Watts. The chorus is:

"At the cross, at the cross where I first saw the light,
And the burden of my heart rolled away,
It was there by faith,
I received my sight,
And now I am happy all the day"

I have a little grandson whose parents are struggling through difficulties. Whenever he would visit, he loved to sing songs he learned in nursery school. Because he loved music and singing, I would sing hymns to him and he loved them. He loved the chorus of "Trust and Obey" where it says, "To be happy in Jesus." He loved the word "happy" in a song. In my car radio, I have a CD I always play of Elvis Presley Gospel music (from 1967).

When grandson rides in the car with me, his favorite song is, "*If the Lord Wasn't Walking by My Side,*" which has "happy" in the lyrics. Some of it is as follows:

"I don't know just what I'd do,
If the Lord wasn't walking by my side.
He heard me praying (he heard me praying on my knees at night).
Now I'm singing (Now I'm singing this happy song).
Because I'm happy (because I'm happy as I go along).
And I don't know (I don't know) just what I'd do,
If the Lord wasn't walking by my side."

There are little common courtesies we do in a day that uplift one another in the home. We can keep each other happy if we work at kindness. But we must remember, it is impossible for us to exude joy if we do not strive to have it in our own hearts. We have to practice, every single day, to stay happy. I love to sing hymns and read hymns because these stay in my mind and bring me peace. They are brought to my mind throughout the day to provide joy and contentment. I am reminded of holy and godly things and this keeps me looking up, instead of all around me.

When my husband goes out of his way to check on me in my homemaking, before he goes off to do a project in the garage, he is showing me kindness. When he asked me if I wanted something special for my birthday this week (even though we don't have the money to waste), he is showing me kindness. He is reminding me to always be happy. In turn, I do the same for him, and for my children, and grandchildren. I serve them in love with sweet manners. But we cannot do any of this in our own strength because trials can destroy our attitude very quickly! We have to be slow and steady in the Lord: - Bible reading, daily prayer, and the singing of hymns must be regular habits in the home to help keep us happy.

We can have joy in the Lord regardless of our circumstances. The key ingredient in this is TRUST. If we trust the Lord with everything in our lives, and know His promises in the Bible, we will draw close to Him for comfort and guidance. This is the greatest form of Happiness in life. We show this by our sweet behavior (in manners and courtesy) to those in our home. This is the fruit of that trust in the Lord.

My husband and I will often say to each other with a gentle, prodding smile, "Are you happy?" or we will say, "Be happy." This is how we remind each other what is truly important. We instantly stop worrying for the moment. It gives us a time of respite to think on the word "happiness!" We know it has everything in the world to do with our level of gratitude to God for our very lives.

Be happy. Be blessed.

58
I Want to Be A Mama

I love when my grandchildren visit me. I will get right up and "make a home" for them. No matter how tired I am, or what I am currently occupied with, I focus on the babies. They are the joy of my life. The other day, my husband noticed I was feeling a little down. In a short period of time after that, I had spoken to all of my grown children on the phone, just briefly. Suddenly I was soaring with happiness. He was amazed to see that if I am near the children, or talking to them for just a little while, it fills me with great joy. This is the blessing of being a mother.

My 4-year-old grand-girl spent part of the day, yesterday, helping me in my domestic life. We were sitting on the couch crocheting. I am about one fourth of the way along making an afghan. She rolls out the yarn as she sits beside me, and we visit. "Who are you making this one for, Me`me?" She asked me. I tell her it is for her brother. "Then, the next one I make will be for you." She is so excited and wants to know what the colors will be. I tell her "pink and purple. But it will take a while. It takes me a long time to make an afghan." She sighs and then says, "Well, I guess I will be helping you forever." She smiles at me. "Every time I visit, I will help you."

She helps me while the family is all around us. Her brothers are playing with puzzles. Someone wants juice. Her Mama is in and out the front door, busy with projects. Grand-girl works with me while we tend the family. We did the dishes, and then the mail was brought in. I am on the list to receive the monthly "King Arthur Flour Catalog." She loves to look through this. There are beautiful pans, delicious looking cakes, decorated cookies, and pizzas! When it was time for the family to go home, they put on all their coats, mittens, boots, and hats. "Don't forget your magazine," I tell her. She tucked it under her arm, with delight, because she gets to keep it. She smiled sweetly and said to me, "When I get big, I want to be a Mama."

59
A New England Winter on a Small Income

We've had our first heavy snowfall, of the season, this morning here in rural Vermont. It is a good day to stay home. I was thinking about Pa and Ma Ingalls and how the family would stay at the homestead and not venture to town on a day like today. In the writings of Laura Ingalls, she would talk about the men using a horse-drawn cutter which, I imagine, is a sled with a sharp base to travel in the snow without difficulty. We would certainly appreciate such transportation here in Vermont!

In the older books of Grace Livingston Hill (such as *"In the Way,"* copyright 1897), the characters are dressed very warm, and are tucked into sleds with thick robes, or wool blankets, for traveling to church and such. (This is an excellent book, by the way, and one of my favorites!)

There is often talk, even in the writings of Charles Dickens in *"Dombey and Son,"* about how one would sit by the warmth of the fire to read or visit. Getting close to the fireplace is how the chill, from outdoors, was soothed.

In modern homes, and businesses, there is central heating which makes the entire building kept at a set temperature to ensure warmth and comfort. But in old houses, such as our 1850's colonial, there is no such thing. Our struggle, and our challenge, each year, is to find ways to keep warm indoors on a small income.

There are many rooms in this humble, old house, over three stories. We also have different sources of heat. Part of our second floor is the least expensive with a wood pellet stove. In some of these rooms there is electric heat, which is unbearably expensive, but necessary at times.

In other rooms, mostly on the main, 1st floor, we have kerosene (which used to be oil) heat. This will keep us very cozy and happy, but it is very expensive at over $3.00 a gallon. If our tank is 200 gallons, and the weather outside is 40 below zero (common on some February days), we will go through a great deal of kerosene (perhaps an entire tank full) in about 3 weeks, if we want to be at a comfortable temperature. But this is not something we can afford to do. So, by comparison of the way people lived, in our readings of old literature, we learn many things of how to stay reasonably warm, in cold New England, at a reasonable cost.

Here are some ideas of what we have learned, living in this chilly, drafty, old house for 15 years:

1. Winter clothes are very important. We cannot walk around the house in summer attire. We need thermals, house coats (robes), and cozy slippers.

2. Papa keeps the thermostat (for kerosene) at 60 degrees in the evenings. During the day he sets it at 63. I get up early and open all

the curtains to get as much natural heat from the sun as possible.

3. We are very hesitant as to when we will first turn on the kerosene heat for the winter. We are also very cautious about how long we can put off that first delivery. This year it happened in October because the cold weather had settled in, right in the middle of autumn. The reason we must be so careful about this is because we only have so much money available for heat, to get through an entire winter season.

4. If we are very cold, Papa will start a fire in our old wood stove in the downstairs kitchen. We have a small table and chairs set up nearby so we can sit and get warm while sipping on hot chocolate. This is also our only source of heat if the electricity goes out. It is so cozy and a blessing to sit by the warmth of a fire!

5. Every doorway, including the one connecting a living room to a kitchen on the first floor, must have an insulated curtain. (I have read that in England, curtains are lined with Flannel to keep houses warm.) We keep these curtains closed so that each room is kept warm. Each room must be closed off from the rest, in order to keep the rooms reasonably warm.

6. Have you ever read of Children in one-room schoolhouses in winter-time? They all pulled their desks close by the wood stove and did their lessons near the source of heat. I don't think anyone would have thought they could keep an entire building warm. One

would have to get near the fireplace, or wood stove, to stay warm.

You also read of families, at home, going upstairs at bedtime to a cold room and snuggling under piles of homemade quilts for warmth. In the morning, Mother or Dad would start a fire in the kitchen stove to start breakfast for the family. This was also a way to warm up the house before they woke up the children, in order for them to get dressed by the fire.

I am grateful for modern heating, but it is not something you find in humble old houses, even today. In our case, we cannot afford to keep our house at 70 degrees. That would be a luxury beyond our means. Our winters last for about 6 months. One would need an entire separate income to keep this old house that cozy. So, we learn from history, to go near the fireplace, or the wood-stove, to take off the chill, as we rest for a little while. Then we get back to our home-keeping work, which also helps keep us warm.

7. When you are sitting too long, and you first get up from under blankets or afghans you will be much colder than normal. Once you start doing some chores, sweeping, putting away laundry, you will warm up. There is no need to turn up the heat unless, you cannot get warm from being active.

8. Whenever I have to travel (to the store or on errands) with Papa driving our car, I bring a warm blanket for my lap so I am extra tucked in and cozy. I have also enjoyed the experience of being in a horse-drawn wagon. We were all tucked in, with thick wool blankets, to keep us nice and warm on a lovely December day, here

in Vermont.

9. Keep a supply of beautiful blankets, and afghans, in all the rooms. We have these on rocking chairs, on the sides of couches, and in chairs by the beds. This provides extra warmth as we sit for our breaks, visit with guests, or when we go to sleep.

10. When we are expecting company, or grandchildren are visiting, I always tell them to dress very warm. "Wear sweaters," I tell them. I also say to put a cozy blanket- sleeper on the babies. In this way, they will be warm, as they play and visit, in our drafty, old house.

I also love to just stay home as much as possible in cold New England. I will do a great deal of reading, sewing, crocheting, and baking. This is time for the indoor home arts. Pretty candles also add an idea of warmth and a sense of cozy ambiance. The warmest room in the house is where you will often find us. This is our front parlour, by the wood pellet stove.

Each year we try to find new ways to keep warm on a small income. Someday, we hope to add another wood pellet stove to the 1st floor. It will be far less expensive than the kerosene. Perhaps this will happen soon?

60
Old Fashioned Revival Hour

I normally watch Dr. Charles Stanley, on DVD, when I exercise in the early morning. This is in our special room on the first floor. My treadmill is right near a set of French doors with a beautiful view of the front grounds. But this room is bitterly cold, in the fall and winter seasons, because there is no heat in there, except the electric baseboards we had installed many years ago. It is too expensive, and frivolous, for me to turn it on just to do my exercise for 30 minutes.

So, my boys moved the treadmill out of that pretty room and into the nearby kitchen. This is a large room on the 1st floor. (It used to be my mother's kitchen when she and Dad lived here with us for 9 years.) Since we don't use this room very often (our working kitchen is upstairs), there is a slight chill, but enough heat to keep the room comfortable.

Since my DVD and television are not easily accessible to me in the old country kitchen, I had to find another way to stay motivated. To fight boredom while walking on the treadmill, I have started listening to The Old Fashioned Revival Hour. This is a radio program, which was hosted by Dr. Charles E. Fuller. It was broadcast during the 1930's through the 1960's. The program includes the singing of beautiful old-time hymns by a quartet and choir. There are sections of readings, and then Dr. Fuller preaches an old-time sermon. These are reminiscent of revivals in the old country churches in the rural south. I love these programs! I have been listening to these each morning while I do my exercises, and use the treadmill.

There is a sermon listing containing such titles as "The Spirit Filled Christian Home;" "Walking in the Light;" "The Hiding Place" (I listened to this one yesterday and it was so good!); "Stand Fast in the Faith:" and "Prayer." I have listened to some of these over and over again. I love to hear the choir singing the old songs like, "*Heavenly Sunlight*" and "*Jesus Saves*" while accompanied by the beautiful sound of the simple, old piano.

This is an amazing way to start the day, with exercise for the body, and precious old-time nourishment for the soul.

61
In the Quiet of the Morning

Here in rural Vermont, it is generally very quiet. There are not many stores around and that adds to the old-fashioned charm of our daily lives. Our 1800's colonial house is full of wonderful memories for me. Great-grandmother and Great-grandfather (my parents) lived here with us for the first 9 years since we bought the house. (They lived in their own section on the first floor.) My five children had some of their growing up years here. Many of my grandchildren have walked up the stairs, holding the banister, since they were toddlers. The hallways and staircases, of this old house, are dear to me.

As I walk through the rooms in the morning, waiting for the sun to rise, I put away some toys the grandchildren left out on their last visit. I fix pillows on the couches. I start opening all the curtains to bring in the first of the early morning light. I pray a prayer of gratefulness for my family and for my humble home, as I step over missing pieces in our kitchen linoleum. Then I start baking muffins.

I think about the little things I will do throughout the day. There is a room that needs to be organized and tidied. My laundry must be started. I plan for the possibility of unexpected guests (such as grown children and grandchildren) by setting up some treats. There are sweet hymns going through my mind that bring happiness to my heart. There is no trouble or trials going on. This is a fresh start, as each new day brings, for all of us. As I work, doing my homemaking duties, in the quiet of the morning, I am at peace.

62
Chores for Grandchildren

When some of my grandbabies were very young, I helped them clean all of their messes. I used to teach them how to do the work. They loved putting their toys away, stacking the story-books, and placing tiny pillows neatly on the bed. They helped me fold towels, washcloths, and pillowcases. I loved to see their efforts at trying to fold the sheets!

They loved to sweep, help with dishes, get their pajamas ready for bath-time, and organize the rooms. I taught them how to make their beds. We made it such fun to do the chores together.

This was when some of the grandchildren (and their mother) lived with us, here at the Estate. It is a large old colonial house with plenty of room for extended family. Now that they are living in their own house, in a nearby town, I do not have as much opportunity to help them clean.

They visit frequently. There are plenty of toys and games for their happy use. I have a nursery (playroom) on the first floor. It is full of fun toys, a baby crib, and a toddler bed. There is a large play area for running, setting up puzzles, building block towers, and racing cars across the room. But there isn't as much time for cleaning.

Often, the children are here for an hour or two and then it is time for them to go home. I had gotten into the habit of forgetting to ask them to clean. This has left me a great deal of work to do alone. It has been wearing me out. I forgot that my little helpers made the work lighter.

Now I am remembering to take plenty of time to have them do the cleaning with me. We are setting up new routines and schedules so they can do chores with Grandmother. We need to stop playing about 30 minutes before they leave. Then we can leisurely work together to make the home look extra nice. This makes them happy and proud of their labor. Once the work is done, we can have a little snack at the table. Or, perhaps we can color and draw together? It is so nice to look around the room and see everything shiny and pretty, knowing that it was because we did all of our chores together. The children learn from this, that working in the home can give us just as much joy as playing.

63
Two Days Off

I have been busy cooking and baking each day. I try to make dinner by five in the evening so I am able to clean everything early before I get too tired. When I am the one who does the cooking and serving, I notice the food lasts much longer. It is important to plan and be careful with our resources. It would be very easy for us to decide to get fast food or a restaurant meal. But this would be incredibly expensive. This is not something that interests us anyway! It saves money for us to make our own meals, but it is also very tiring work. Sometimes, however, our grown children like to get restaurant food. I cringe at the money they spend!

Last week, I had an unexpected treat. Our youngest son (in his 20's) decided to try out some recipes. He wanted to use the kitchen. He explained that he was going to make two desserts and two dinners. He was to do all the work alone. He took a small amount of his savings and bought the groceries himself. I stayed in my room, reading a book, delighted for a rest. I was so grateful he was not wasting money on take-out food.

Every so often, he would pop in and ask me a question. "Where is the measuring cup?" He would ask. Or, "Do you have any flour?" I was happy to help and then get back to my reading. It was not long before he had made both the desserts and finished the first night's dinner. I was so surprised to see how clean and neat everything was.

He took the time to save the food after the meal and to do all the dishes. It was the same on the 2nd night. He made the dinner and then washed and cleaned everything. Then I remembered that he had spent 2 years working in an Inn and Restaurant, a few years ago. He has a couple of certificates from culinary training. He just never really took the time to use my kitchen. He did a wonderful job. (His older brother is a chef, and kitchen manager, at the Inn, and has worked there for more than 5 years.)

I enjoyed my two days off. It is a blessing that others in the family enjoy the work of cooking and cleaning in the kitchen. But I do have to share the sweetest of all. During the 1st night of his cooking, he came into my room, sat down for a rest, and said to me, "how do you do all this work every night??" I was delighted!

64
A Sweet Little Visitor

Our tenth little grandbaby came to stay with us for a while. She was born at the very end of August. Her mother is one of my daughters. I picked them both up at the city hospital and drove the long 2 - hour drive back to my house. My daughter was recovering from a cesarean and needed extra care. As soon as I heard I was needed to get them, I quickly got to work on the guest room.

A television was placed on the dresser. Baby's Mother would need to be resting a great deal of the time and would enjoy watching some programs. I also took a rocking chair out of my bedroom and placed it in the guest room. She would need to gently rock the baby and use the chair to rest in during feedings. The hospital had a grant program and gave all new mothers a brand-new portable crib for free. This sweet bed would be placed in the guest room for baby. I took one of our tray tables to put beside the rocking chair. The guest bed was made. It looked inviting and cozy. The room was all ready for them when we arrived back home.

For the next several days, I gave up my morning exercise routine to take care of our guests. I was busy, early each morning, washing and sterilizing bottles from the night feedings. I would get up at 5 a.m. just to make sure a fresh batch of bottles would be ready for the day. In the late evenings, I did the washing and sterilizing again before I went to bed.

I provided mother with a basin of warm water for sponge baths. I just happened to have baby bath and baby lotion for just such an occasion! One never knows when a baby might be visiting. One ought to have all necessary supplies! Our treasure smelled so very precious after her sweet little baths.

I never asked to hold the baby. I remember how much I loved having my own babies with me at all times. I did not want to take away any of that joy from baby's mother. I also knew that there would be moments when Mother would say, "Can you hold the baby while I take a shower?" Or, "Would you hold the baby while I get something to eat?" I was always ready to stop whatever I was doing for the joy of holding our sweet little visitor.

I spent my days enjoying the family, listening to the precious sounds of baby, and keeping the home tidy. I loved going into the guest room and quietly asking, "Do you need anything?" Or, I would say, "How is baby?" The response was always a smile and an invitation into the room. I delighted in having such wonderful company in our home.

One day, some of the little cousins came to visit. They had no idea there was a new baby. The little, 5-year-old girl spotted a car seat in the living room and asked about it. I told her, "There is a new baby here." Her eyes lit up with delight! She looked at me and said, "Show me!" She was stunned! We brought baby into the room. She was so happy to see that her Aunt had a new baby. The children took turns sitting on the couch so they could carefully hold their new little cousin.

My daughter's recovery went very quickly. She needed to get back to the city to be near her own doctor and baby's doctor. A day was arranged for me to drive them back home. We stopped whenever necessary, on the long drive, so she could take care of baby. When it was time to say goodbye, it was so hard for me. I knew I would dearly miss them. When I got back home, I saw the empty guest room, and cried. But each day, my daughter sent me pictures and stories about their days. I was comforted. I realized I was thankful for the opportunity to have them here for that short period of time. I had not expected to be needed! I am especially grateful for such a precious time with my special visitors.

65
Pacing Oneself to Keep House

I do not have a maid to help me keep house. There is no staff of workers to cook, bake, clean, decorate, and organize. There is no accountant to keep the finances in order. I do not have a hostess to welcome and care for guests and residents here at our Estate. Groceries are not delivered. The shopping and errands and the management of the entire household is not completed by a head-housekeeper. Most homemakers do all of these things, and much more. They do it alone.

There is a way to do these things, in a gentle, gracious way. I will share with you just two common ideas. They are basic and ordinary, but can make all the difference:

----

1. **Keep a Weekly Schedule.**

If you do the shopping on Wednesday (for example), the heavy cleaning on Thursday, the Laundry on Friday, etc. You will not be trying to do it all in one day. If some emergency happens, or you are not feeling well, you can just do the basics and not worry about it.

If I am going to bake homemade bread on Tuesday, I will not go out on errands. That would be too much of a drain on my energy. If I am going to deep clean the house on Thursday, I will not make homemade pizza. We have to balance the heavy and light work for each day. This is part of pacing ourselves to do the many different tasks in a day.

2. **Keep a Daily Routine.**

I believe the most time-consuming work, each day, happens in the kitchen! Pace yourself to have the energy and the peace to prepare these meals. (If you have children who are old enough to help you, all the better! It is a joyful time to prepare and serve food with the family's help.)

There are three meals prepared and served each day. Many homemakers provide the family with easy food for breakfast and lunch. The main meal of the day is often served at the dinner hour. It is the old, traditional "supper time," where all the family is home together for the evening meal. This will vary in each home, depending on the family schedule. For example: If Dad works the night shift, perhaps the family enjoys a big breakfast or lunch together.

If we kept a daily journal of all the things we do in a day, it would make us tired! Yet in the midst of all the work, we can have many moments of laughter, tea breaks, walks about the garden, times for reading and resting, and just enjoying family visits in the parlour. We can learn, through practice, to do all the work of "keeping house" in a gentle way, by avoiding stress, rush, worry, and fear.

Think on that which is good, and pretty, and pleasant. Focus on the beauty around us. Be grateful. Be courageous when you are weary. Rest as often as necessary. Pace yourself with little simple jobs, with plenty of tea breaks, seeking contentment and joy in home life.

66
The Day I Quit Gardening

I have always considered myself an amateur gardener. I struggle with doing the work, and find myself constantly distracted by other things - like butterflies, pretty wild-flowers, and listening to the birds.

Each summer I have tried to do a little bit of gardening. I take it slow. Often, I only attempt to grow cucumbers, which I love for summer salads and tea sandwiches. But always we have our strawberries and blueberries, which provide us with a small harvest, despite my lack of effort.

This is not because I am lazy. It is not because I lead a pampered life. It is because I am enjoying the work indoors. I am baking, vacuuming, dusting, making homemade food, visiting with the family, mending in the parlour, and being a gracious hostess to our frequent guests - who are mostly our grown children and our precious grandchildren. I am reading stories to little ones, getting juice and snacks, or I am folding the laundry and taking breaks to read a lovely story that gives me a time of rest and recreation.

I have noticed that my walks outside, on our two acres, are an incredible respite from all I am doing inside. I love to see the river behind our land. It is often raging and high in the spring, but low and peaceful in summer.

I am often drawn to this area of the grounds. I will stare at the rushing river and watch as there are waterfalls among the rocks.

I was starting to miss these little walks that brought me great happiness. Our cucumber garden has been flourishing all season. I was gathering the berries and then the many cucumbers that seemed to be more numerous than I could manage. (I was giving away bags of this to some of my grown children.) Each day, it seemed, there was more work than I could manage. I am not one who has ever learned to "can" or preserve what we grow. Honestly, I struggle enough to do my regular work and spend time resting with the family. I do not have the strength to do much more. I do not *want* to do more.

One morning, I became so stressed about the abundant crop of cucumbers, and realizing I could not keep up with all the labor, that I sat down with my husband and said, "I just cannot do this anymore." He smiled. He knew I was doing too much, but he thought I had been enjoying the work. I had not been. I said, with a relieved smile, "so I quit." And that was settled. I will not let myself feel guilty. Someday I might change my mind. But for now, I do not have to be a gardener.

We will certainly continue with our berries. Perhaps my husband will do his own gardening next season since he enjoys being busy outdoors. We have even discussed planting a few more pretty flowers, like the miniature parade roses that are near our front porch. I would like to have beautiful things on the grounds, that do not mind neglect, as I walk around the property, to rest from all my labor indoors.

I am thankful for the food I can purchase at my local store. I can fill up my pantry with sale items and find the most nutritious options to bring home. I can "gather our food from afar," and not try to do it all on my own. I appreciate the farmers and the gardeners that do all this labor for those of us who are not able. This is a blessing and a relief. I am grateful to have this option!

{Note – The following year, my husband took over all the gardening.}

67
Peaceful Homemaking

Lately, I have been too tired to do the shopping. I have been running low on many supplies for the kitchen. Each day I would think, "well I better go to the store tomorrow." But somehow, I came up with an idea of what to bake and cook so I could stay at home. I was too weary to do errands. I wanted to put off the shopping as long as possible. I am also struggling with the grocery money this month. So many bills come to us in the Fall months. We just paid our annual property taxes. The insurance on the house needs to be taken care of in the coming weeks. I need to save up for these big expenses. I have to make do with what I have on hand, as much as possible, right now.

In order to save money, I have been extra busy in the kitchen. One day I made homemade Italian bread to go with a simple spaghetti dinner. The fresh baked bread helps fill everyone up. It was a great deal of work but we all enjoyed it very much.

I baked muffins, brownies, and a simple white cake. There was always some kind of home-baked treat for the family. I love homemade food, especially to enjoy during tea breaks.

Through all the work, I find the greatest happiness in hearing precious old-time sermons on my kitchen radio. I have a CD by Dr. Clyde Box, called, "*A Faithful Man- Who Can Find?*" This is old southern preaching. I also listen to Dr. Charles Stanley. I love the beautiful, inspiring words that give one an incredible sense of peace and joy in life. This is what I look forward to doing while I am baking, and cooking, and cleaning: - Hearing the old gospel preaching that comforts the soul.

Each morning I wonder what I can cook for the family. Each day I am amazed that even though I have no money in my purse this week, the Lord helps me come up with an idea of what I can make from my limited pantry. I have not been in need at all, and I am so thankful.

My grown children and grandchildren visit me often. I love offering them food from my kitchen. I will happily cook, and bake, and work hard to give them comfort and happiness. Food makes us happy! It is a blessing! Even though we live simply and do not have very much, I am grateful.

These days, I think we need encouragement in trusting God for our daily bread. I think we need to focus on our homemaking and be careful with what we already have in the pantry. Our culture seems to constantly distract us into doing projects that are the latest trend, or that we should be buying the latest gadget, or trying out the latest new recipe. All the while, we are overwhelmed with ads and commercials. These things should not consume our everyday thinking. It will take away our feeling of contented peace. I would love to read more about homemakers who are just peacefully, and sweetly, keeping the home.

I love remembering the old days of my childhood. My mother always made a good dinner each night at the same time. It was the quiet hour of the day. The world was shut out for a time. I always felt safe and comforted to be home. I hope we mothers of today can give that same feeling to our own families.

68
Treats from the Kitchen

I have been doing a lot of baking. I try to keep a steady supply of homemade brownies, cookies, or coffee cake in my kitchen. I love to offer treats for the family. One afternoon, I had baked a "frozen" apple pie and was busy preparing a batch of brownies. One of my grown sons came into the room and gratefully said, "Why are you always making desserts?" I thought it was so sweet. He is my biggest fan and just loves all the fresh baked goods.

I think we have gotten used to having snacks and treats these days that it is nice to be able to bake and cook them ourselves. They are going to be much healthier if they are homemade instead of the convenience food version from the grocery store. It is also such a blessing to enjoy the delightful scent of fresh baked treats from the kitchen.

Some of my grandchildren are my frequent visitors. As soon as they walk in the door, one or two will always say, "Did you bake muffins today?" It is one of their favorite treats to have Me`me's homemade muffins.

Late at night, after I have gone to sleep, I know my husband will visit the kitchen and help himself to brownies or cookies. It makes him smile to think they have been specially made for the family to enjoy.

I also love when there are guests who visit (mostly my grown children and grandchildren) and I have some special food to offer them. "Would you like a piece of pie?" I might ask. These treats often tempt a lagging appetite, and bring some happiness to their day.

Food is such a blessing, and we are so grateful for what the Lord has given us. It will always be my favorite thing to bake, and cook, little treats in my humble kitchen.

69
Getting a Fire in the Morning

We had a dreadfully cold morning the other day. Normally, we are all piled with blankets to keep us warm, but getting out of bed is a challenge when the air is cold. This is why a warm, cozy fire is a necessity.

My husband doesn't get a lot of sleep, because of his disabled condition. So, he is often awake and in the downstairs living room most of the time. On this cold morning, I put on a couple of house robes and ventured down the stairs. "Could I have a fire?" I sweetly asked him. He always gets right up and comes to my aid.

Our wood pellet stove is the main source of heat for the second floor, right next to our bedroom. (The rest of the house is heated by Oil or Kerosene.) I went right back to bed until the rooms warmed up from the cozy fire, he set up for me.

It reminded me of my father's boyhood days. He and his older brother shared a bedroom. Their father would call out, in the early morning hours, for one of them to get up and do the fire. It was a normal chore for farm families in the old days. Nobody wanted to get out of bed until that nice fire had warmed up the house. I love that my father and his brother were required to take turns doing the work. It helped to make them responsible and hardworking men, who later took excellent care of their own families.

For me to be cold, and have other hardships in daily life, makes me so incredibly grateful for every little blessing. I realize modern heating and cooling makes life so much more pleasant. We do not often notice how much effort it used to take to get warm, or cool, depending on the season. But I love that little touch of chilling, cold that reminds me to be thankful. It reminds me of the old days.

In my own childhood home, we had a large fireplace in the living room. It was always so cozy and comforting when Dad got up a good fire to keep us warm. This is essential warmth in our dear old New England. There is nothing quite like a good fire to take away the chill in the air.

It did not take my husband long to get the wood pellet stove working. The warmth radiated throughout the rooms and made the temperature comfortable for me. I was able to do my morning work of getting a little breakfast and doing some cleaning. Then I sat by the "hearth" for a little tea, and a rest, and was grateful for the blessing of home.

70
School Work for Grandmother

We have two little grandchildren who are enrolled in a Christian school. They love doing homework and have been so happy to show me their papers. Whenever they visit me, I provide them with a variety of tools at the table. These include crayons, pencils, paper, and rulers. They get busy playing school, making homework papers, and creating puzzles and mazes.

One afternoon, five-year-old grand-girl called me to the table. She reached for my hand and said, "Me`me, I am going to teach you how to write your letters." I was delighted. She had used a ruler to set up lines and draw little marks and letters for me to trace. This little girl is the only one in our entire family who is "left-handed." She has struggled a little bit in school as she has been learning to do her writing. I thought this would be a perfect opportunity for me to discreetly give her a little guidance. In order to do this, I decided to only use my left hand. Clearly, it would cause me to write like a small child and would be difficult. But it would also allow me to get on her level and understand how to teach her.

As I traced the prepared letters, I explained how and what I was doing. Just a little word of wisdom here, with an example, and another word of wisdom there, helped tremendously. Soon she was testing out my ideas on another paper and improving her own writing.

Sometimes, I would ask the 1st grader (her older brother) what a certain cursive letter was supposed to look like. I wanted to be certain I was doing the work the same way the school wanted it done. He proudly demonstrated each time I asked. It was a wonderful help.

At each visit, both the students gave me homework to do. It was not long before I was filling in missing letters, giving addition and subtraction answers, circling the largest number, solving puzzles, and giving hints on "place value" in math. It was mentally tiring for me, but brought tremendous delight for the children, as they continued to make me many pages of school work.

I have homeschooled my children throughout their entire education. It was wonderful to be able to work with some of my grandchildren. These sweet grand-babies are having a great deal of fun with just papers, pencils, and rulers. It has become a wonderful part of their visits, to teach their Me`me how to do homework.

71
Keep Traditions Alive

This Thanksgiving was expected to be a small affair. All my grown children were either working, had plans with extended family, or were unable to travel home. This was hard to adjust to at first, but in the last couple of years, I have gotten used to this and understand. We see each other whenever we can. We also talk on the phone as much as possible.

But whether everyone is here for the day, or it is just two of us for the dinner, I want to keep the traditions alive. I have a beautiful set of white gravy bowls with pretty white lids. Each one sits on a matching gold stand. These belonged to my grandmother. My Mother would fill both with gravy and place one on each end of the large table for the family gathering. This makes things extra special. I only use one of the bowls at my table, since there are not as many people here to enjoy the meal.

I love to decorate my sideboard table with a pretty tablecloth. We often set up serving bowls, or all the desserts, on this table. My mother always did this too. She would use a large kitchen counter, or set up another table, to display some of the wonderful food. It helped create the holiday! We mothers have to do the extra work and care to make things look pleasant and inviting. There ought to be a sense of the different, a sense of awe, to see that this is a special day of celebration.

I got up extra early to put the turkey in the oven. Someone gets up with me every year to help. One of my girls would usually help me. Then my husband started to help. This year, since we had a smaller turkey, I tried to do it alone. But when I got up before the sun, and reached in to take the turkey out of the refrigerator, I had to laugh because I could not lift it! I had to go and wake up my husband. He was happy to come to my aid. We worked together to do the little tasks of preparation and then got it into the oven. This helping me with the turkey is part of the tradition. The older children will say, "Who will help Mom with the turkey?" I love that they worry and care that someone is always here to help me.

I set a pretty table with a cloth tablecloth, our dishes, cloth napkins, and a pretty candle. This is part of doing the same special things each year. We present our best for holidays and special occasions. We do the extra work in baking, and cooking, and decorating, to make things look lovely, even in a humble, old fashioned way.

My father presided over our Thanksgiving table for many years. He always said the sweetest prayers. I felt so grateful and honored to hear them. He and Mother lived with us, here in our Vermont home, for 9 years. They moved south when the cold winter weather became too much for them. I asked Dad if he would please write out a prayer, for our first Thanksgiving here on our own. He hesitated. He didn't feel it was right to write it out. But I begged and pleaded. I wanted his prayer to continue to be a part of our Tradition. He finally agreed and mailed it to me. (Sadly, he passed away a few months later.) Since then, I have read his handwritten prayer at all our Thanksgiving dinners. I am always so grateful for this!

This year, my husband and I thought we would do all our simple traditions alone. But we were surprised and delighted to find that our two grown sons had evening shifts at work, and would both be able to enjoy the food with us. I prepared an early dinner. It was all ready before the noon hour and we had a lovely time of visiting at our Thanksgiving table.

It is up to we mothers to keep up the work of pleasant traditions. It is a beautiful work, and a wonderful way of passing the years, bringing happiness, and pleasant memories, into our homes. This will bring our children and grandchildren a great deal of joy! It will also bless Mother and Dad, especially when the time comes when their dinners are spent quietly serving just two.

72
The Organized Home

I used to love reading books written by Emilie Barnes. She was so encouraging in keeping a pleasant, tidy home. Her tips for doing little, 15-minute organizing jobs were wonderful. Her books were always beautifully decorated and full of practical, calming encouragement.

These days, the fashion is to get rid of everything, or to live a minimalistic life. Frankly, this does not interest me. I get sad when I see a home with almost nothing around. I want to see homemade afghans over the couch. I love to see pretty pictures on the walls. I want to see lovely curtains that look feminine and frilly, with white lace in the background! I want to see pretty things that make a home look comforting and pleasant. I want home to be a place of beauty, with lovely things all around.

But I do not like to see piles of clutter, or a bunch of junk that nobody wants to have around. We do need to keep things organized and orderly. We most certainly should discard items we no longer want to keep. But we should be practicing the art of cleaning and organizing.

There is another book, I used to enjoy reading, that helps with keeping the home nice. It is called, *"Sidetracked Home Executives."* The authors (sisters) have such a fun sense of humor. The book was full of funny, cartoon illustrations as well. The book was inspiring and fun to read. It encouraged the daily work of organizing and managing the home. This will always be an important part of homemaking.

I often need a reminder, or some motivation, to get back on track to keep all the rooms looking nice and tidy. My desk and bureau become frequent spots for clutter to accumulate. I get too busy with other things to remember to put everything away, or to throw out the junk mail and mail - order catalogs. This is why I try to keep one day each week for the purpose of organizing.

I don't think I am the type who can do the 15-minute jobs of tidying. I get too busy with many distractions, and the needs of the family. That is why, for me, I need an entire day devoted to the work of organizing. In this way, I can get sidetracked, distracted, or called away, and still have plenty of time, throughout the day, to accomplish some of the work of tidying.

A pretty, organized home takes time. It is an ongoing job that should be fun. It is like "playing house" and "decorating." It is something we should enjoy, and make a part of our weekly routine. This will help our homes to stay lovely and pleasant.

73
The Boarding School

I set up a row of little beds, with nice pillows and comforters, in one of the larger bedrooms in our house. I cleared out a room for toys, and baskets of clothes and laundry. We were getting ready to open up a boarding school for our four sweet children (who were homeschooled). I had all the school books neatly stacked in a bookcase, in careful piles. A card table and highchairs were set up in the parlour, near our main dining room table, for morning classes. I was to teach grades preschool, kindergarten, first, and second grade (ages 3 to 8), to four of my grandchildren. I was delighted!

The children arrived one afternoon, at the beginning of the month. They had plenty of toys, games, books, and lots of rooms in this house to enjoy. We were to start our little school the next morning, the day their baby brother was to be born. They were to stay with me for a few weeks, while their Mother recovered from a surgical childbirth.

We rose at 6 a.m. I could hear the quiet chatter of the children, and knew morning had come. While I got the table ready for their breakfast, they made their little beds. Often, one of the dear ones would sneak over and make my bed too.

I separated the children, in groups of two, at the different tables. I would call the younger two, "the preschool and kindergarten class," at the card table; and the older two, "the 1st and 2nd grade class" at the main table. There was plenty of room for them to do their math, reading, writing, spelling, and handwriting. We started our school with Bible devotions and prayer. I read from a darling, little picture book called, *"The One Year Devotions for Preschoolers 2"* by Carla Barnhill. It had the most charming illustrations, and sweet, and simple Bible lessons. Then we got right to work.

I worked with each child, on all their lessons, as I walked back and forth in the room. The older children had an abacus, and special learning clocks, to help with their math lessons. We had stacks of blank paper for any extra help, or illustrations I needed to write out, to help them learn.

Often, I would be doing a little baking, or dishes, in the attached kitchen, while they were busy doing their worksheets. One day, a few of the children needed my help at once, as I was putting a batch of muffins in the oven. I rushed over to help. The oldest said, "It must be hard, teaching four grades, and baking at the same time." They were so sweet and patient with me.

At times, a sensitive child had made a mistake in a writing or math lesson. I had to gently point out how to fix the error. Instead of saying, "this is wrong." I would say, "I am not sure if this is the right answer." They took this kindly and were happy to fix the mistake. This helped them to learn to check their work, proofread, and understand how to find the answers on their own. If they could not figure it out, I taught them how to find the answer. "Do not worry," I would say. "School is not easy. It is a lot of hard work, and you are doing a great job!"

I had the joy and privilege of watching them soar, and improve, in all their skills over the course of many days. I gave the older grades math drill pages (with 100 problems) each day. It was difficult at first, but they enjoyed the challenge. The 1st grader used a wooden abacus. I could hear her quietly singing her math problems, as she moved the wooden beads, and wrote down her answers. She would sing, "3 minus 1 equals 2. . . 4 minus 3 equals 1." She did not notice anyone around her, as she quietly sang the problems, to herself, as she solved each one. After many days, she was so happy to announce that she no longer needed the abacus. She told us she was getting so good at this! It was not long before she quickly completed all 100 problems, in a short period of time, and loved the work.

The children helped me with the daily chores. We folded their laundry and put it all away. They set and cleared the table, swept the floor, and washed the table after meals. Each afternoon, we went outside to the playground on the side of our property. They loved riding on the swings, going down the slide, and running in the grass. Then we went inside to the playroom so they could build with blocks, or play with cars and puzzles. They colored each day and drew many pictures. Throughout all my work of taking care of them and making meals, I kept a little baggie of M & M candies in my apron pocket. They would often catch me sneaking a little treat. When they spotted me, I would get them each one: - Of the color of their choice.

In the evenings, the older two children would each give me their own Bibles. I would always read Psalm 117 from one Bible, and Psalm 100 from the other Bible. They each wanted me to read something from their own beloved book. I did this every single night before bed. Then we would say a bedtime prayer and all would be tucked into bed for a good night's sleep. I was so grateful to be able to take care of them all. I loved them dearly.

Each morning, I would pray to the Lord to, "Please give me patience today." He always answered my prayer. I was calm and patient and very blessed. The children were easy to take care of, mostly because I love them so much. I expected to be tired. I expected to give up everything else I had been doing, and just focus on them. I expected there to be noise, and occasional whining, or disagreements among the children. This, to me, was normal and part of childhood. Because of all this, I did not really hear their noise. I thought they were all perfect angels. That must be how all grandmothers feel.

The children went back home after three and a half weeks. They were so happy to be with their new baby brother! (This was my 12th grandchild!) I visited them every single day, back at their own home, to help take care of them, and continue our schoolwork. And while the adjustment for me, of missing them, was painfully sad, our time of running a little boarding school will always remain in my memories, as a very precious gift.

74
Chasing Butterflies

It is a common sight to see young children enjoying the quiet beauty of nature. They love to look at flowers, trees, plants, and tiny bits of grass. The sight and sound of birds, above, are their delight. On the rare occasion, in the summer months, when they see a butterfly, they start to chase it. Butterflies, here on our Vermont grounds, are greatly attracted to the lilacs. The children will stare and smile and look on, in gentle innocence, at the antics of beautiful butterflies. This is simple innocence. It is a manner of living, in little children, of peace and happiness, regardless of what is going on in the world. It is an enviable way to live.

I have learned to keep that gentle innocence in my older years. When someone, around me, talks of calamity, worry, stress, and pain going on in the world, I want to quickly move my thoughts to butterflies and flowers. I want to think of the great and lovely creations of the Lord, that bring peace and joy, and keep my heart on Heavenly thoughts. I call this "chasing butterflies."

It is a way to find joy in the midst of trouble. It is a way to see sunlight streaming through a dangerous storm. It is hope and happiness while suffering through some difficulty.

I will give you an example of this type of living: This month, one of my grown sons needed medical attention. It was not a major ailment, but he clearly needed medical direction and assistance. We were not able to get an appointment at our local doctor's office. We decided it would be best to go to the Emergency Room. My son has such good sense of humor and we had a lovely drive to the Hospital. It happened to be very early in the morning. There was a stunning dimness as the sun was coming up. A gentle rain, and a bit of fog, lingered at the end of an overnight storm. I could not help pointing out the beauty of the morning as I drove along. He gently reminded me to "watch the road." He was patient with my awe and comments of the beauty of the sky, and mountain view, as we drove along. I told him that, on any other normal drive, I would have pulled the car over to stop and take pictures. But I knew we needed to get him to the hospital and I would get him there safely.

As we came around a curve, there appeared in front of us, a large and glorious rainbow! I could not contain myself. This was the comfort of God! This was a privilege and a blessing to see! We were both stunned and grateful. We were soon at the Hospital and all was well. But this amazing experience of beauty and nature truly calms and delights us with Heavenly thoughts. It gets us through the hard times.

I will always strive to be one who "chases butterflies," even at the craziest moment. I will seek and search out the pretty things in life that give me joy and peace, and a contentment that passeth all understanding, especially in difficult trials.

75
Every Day is a Gift

One of the greatest things I have ever learned is that every day is a gift. I am thankful, each morning, to have been given another day. We are to "take no thought for the morrow." This means, to me, that I must not worry. I must not borrow burdens and troubles from future days, or play the game of "what if?" People frequently try to ask me that question. They will say, "What would you do if....?" I respond, content, and with peace, the same answer each time. "I do not play the 'what if' game." I will not let myself answer in any other way. It gets dropped, and the conversation is directed to something more pleasant and productive.

To trust in the Lord for each moment brings peace. This takes a great deal of practice. We must know that we, His dear precious children, are here to do whatever work He calls upon us to do, which is a joy. He will take care of us in all things. As long as we seek to remember that, why should we worry? This takes away much of the possibility for disappointment. There is no desire for ambition.

How precious, to simply want to do the Master's work. We can say a little prayer, much like the missionary, "What is today's work, dear Lord? I am happy to do it." We follow His ways, read the Bible, sing hymns, and do all for the glory of God. This is the best and greatest use of time. Each day is, most certainly, a gift.

76
Keep Rebuilding the Home

Some people are suffering through a great deal of crisis. A lot of young families have been struggling off-and-on for years to build a family and live a happy, stable life, in this very difficult world. It seems like this is very common to many homes in these modern days. Many want to give up on it all, give in to their circumstances, wear out, and struggle through a life of misery. Throughout our lives, any one of us can face this kind of obstacle. But we must keep rebuilding the home.

We have to work on relationships. Each day we must show kindness and good manners. We need dignity and an ability to remain calm throughout the daily troubles. Keep doing those little things that build a bond of trust and love within the family.

We have to manage our finances in the best possible way. In times of high costs of food, heat, and transportation, we have to learn to be creative, get by, and do our best to remain hopeful. We must try to remain cheerful, trusting God, even in the face of job layoffs, sickness, and unexpected bills.

If we are doing our best to manage the money, when trouble comes, we can rest content, knowing we did our best. We must have the assurance and faith that God will provide the rest.

Spread cheer and happiness. One of the greatest medicines of all is that of laughter. This lightens the heart and lessens the pressure of burdens. In this day of panic attacks, stress on levels of high- alert, and out-of-control depression, we need to find a joyous sense of happiness to get us through these times of turmoil. This can only come with a yielding of ourselves to the care of our Heavenly Father. If we trust Him with all things, our burden is light. The result is happiness and peace. This can easily show forth in a lighthearted sense of humor, which can keep us all cheerful.

Several days this month, I helped an extended relative get through some very difficult times. I visited every day, bringing hot homemade soup, fresh baked goods, and whatever else I could, to be certain all were being fed. Some needed a renewed sense of purpose. Sometimes when one is living in a state of despair, a few necessary items to brighten their life will draw them out of their misery, and awaken them again to the joy in living.

We made plans to clean and fix up the little house they owned. Each day we went to a local store to buy paint supplies, or some inexpensive piece of hardware, to fix up the home. I had a careful, modest, budget available to buy urgent needs, which included new pillows, blankets, and fresh supplies for the bathroom. A new shower curtain was put into place. Fresh bath rugs, in bright cheerful colors, were laid out on a newly scrubbed floor. Some things were brought over from my own home to help in the effort. We worked on several of the rooms, and the porch, to be certain the occupants had some productive things to keep their minds off their troubles. One day, when my relative was feeling dangerously low in spirit, I whisked them off to a local furniture store to just browse, walk around, and dream of better ways of living. We did not have any money, but we needed to dream of better days and possibilities! One did not need to dwell, or wallow, in bad times. We needed to keep rebuilding the home!

There were days that I worked so hard helping this relative that I became unbearably weary. The thought came to my mind, again and again, what others may be thinking: "Why are you doing all this? They are just going to ruin it all again, and get back to their old troubles, in a very short time. Why are you wearing yourself out with this? Why spend time and money when it may all get ruined again?" I did not care. That was not my concern. What we did "today" was helping "today." It did not matter if it got ruined tomorrow, or next week. This was doing a precious work to help my relative get through very bad days.

When those thoughts came, I quickly said a prayer that all the necessary effort would be useful. That was all that mattered. I remembered a quote I have on my living room wall, by Mother Theresa. It is called, "Do It Anyway." It encouraged and comforted me. Because we must remember that the work of building up the home, and family, are the greatest things we can do, day after day, month after month, and year after year. We do not seek results. We leave that in God's hands.

After several weeks, my relative was on the mend. They were back on track and better than ever. Many blessings came along to help smooth the troubled road. It was not long before I could rest content, back in my own home, knowing all was well again. It had all been worth the effort. God provided the desired results. We were grateful.

The world and its troubles will be a continual assault to destroy the home and family. We are so much stronger if we have a godly family bond to keep us going. The family, and the home, is a blessed gift from God. We must continue to take care of it all. Just remember to never give up, the daily work, of rebuilding the home.

77
Finding Warmth by the Fire

In the early weeks of autumn, there is a looming chill that sets into our little, Vermont village. It warns of bitterly cold winter days ahead. We spend many months saving up and preparing for the necessary cost of heat. I am most grateful for our wood pellet stove, which sits in the parlour, on the second floor, of our drafty, old house. It brings forth such a cozy heat that I am comforted on difficult days.

In years past, my husband did all the work of caring for the stove. I would walk downstairs to our living room, on cold mornings, and ask, "Would you turn the heat on for me?" He would happily get up and attend to this necessary work. He cleaned out the stove, each day, and set it up, to go back on again, whenever I needed its warmth. This happened morning, and evening, throughout the long winter months.

Last year, he tried to teach me how to use the program buttons to adjust the blower speed, turn on the unit, and handle an apparent trouble, when a strange code appeared that needed an adjustment. I was always afraid of breaking such an important unit, that I was not able to do the work without his help. This required him to come to my aid several times a week, to do simple, basic things, just to provide heat for the second floor.

Somehow, a sense of bravery and confidence overcame me when I saw how much my husband was suffering (because of his disability) each time he used the stairs. I realized I could relieve some of his burden, if I just tried to trust myself enough to learn to use the machine. At first, I waited until he was awake in the morning before I turned on the unit. I was concerned about an error code appearing, which would lead me to panic. This did not happen. Day after day, I managed to turn the machine off and on, and adjust the blower speed, without trouble.

Then, one late afternoon, the dreaded error code finally appeared. I called downstairs to him. He happened to be very weary and was hesitant to walk upstairs while he was in such pain. He asked if I could manage the buttons to fix the error. His gentle trust and instructions helped tremendously. He came upstairs and sat beside me, on the couch, as we watched to see if the lighted code would correct itself. He reassured me that all would be well. I soon learned not to worry, and was no longer afraid.

What a relief this must have been for him to have me manage such simple work this winter season! I did not realize how easy it was to operate the unit, even when my hands are shaking and I am overtired. It was a blessing.

Now on cool autumn mornings, I can quietly sit by the light of the stove. I sit on the parlour couch and have hot tea with a lemon wedge. I have a delicious homemade muffin and read an old time, inspiring book. It is a wonderful, cozy time of having breakfast by the fire.

78
Cheering Up the Home
(2020)

As soon as we saw the first snow, here in Vermont, I wanted to do special things to cheer up the home. My husband set up the Christmas lights on our garage and front porches. He set out our little, 6 - foot tree, on a stand, in the center of the front grounds. These Christmas decorations help brighten the mood and make me smile.

One afternoon, I had to go to the pharmacy. I wandered around the aisles of Christmas displays as I waited for the prescription to be ready. I had just a few dollars and hoped to find something special. I found a beautiful coaster with a charming winter scene. It was only $3.00. This sits on a tea table in my room. It brings me a bit of joy.

With all the worry and stress going on around us, I am focusing on the home instead of on the news. I am busy with the family and homemaking and trying to bring peace and stability to our lives, despite the fear of our times. Right now, it is the season of Thanksgiving and Christmas. There are many precious days ahead.

I have been looking at photo albums and treasures from parents and grandparents. They have lived through many rough days, just as we are living through ours. But the heritage of home, making a cheerful and restful place for the family, has always been the priority throughout the generations.

I am planning little gift ideas for our 12 grandchildren. I am thinking about the Christmas fudge and cookies I will make to give to the families of my grown children. I will listen to old gospel music, precious sermons, and wonderful, old fashioned Christmas music on my kitchen CD- player.

After my husband set up the lights and the tree, I had to go out on an errand. It was not yet nightfall when I left. Some of my errands are stressful, as shopping and banking are full of reminders of a virus we cannot see. These are tiring days, but the work must go on. After I finished the shopping, the sun began to set. The Vermont landscape was so peaceful. As I drove along, I remembered the Christmas lights at home. I had hoped my husband would have them all turned on, for me to see when I returned. Soon I was driving towards our house. I was delighted to see the lights. It was so cheerful, and fun, and happy to see something so beautiful, despite what is going on in the world around us.

Every day, if we could only find some way of cheering up our surroundings, bringing laughter and joy into our home, and helping to boost morale, as we trudge through this life. It is certainly an adventure. Despite all the trials and troubles, we can create moments of happiness. Mother and Dad are often the ones to make the home a memorable and wonderful place to be. We can do this no matter what is going on in the world. We can protect the home and guard our families, bringing them joy and blessings, with the help of our dear Lord.

79

A Humble Thanksgiving

This Thanksgiving will be a simple one for us. I am used to large family gatherings with grandparents, children, and grandchildren. Last year was the first small dinner with only my husband and I, along one little grand-baby, to enjoy the meal. This year it may only be two of us that will be here. Sometimes my grown children may surprise me and visit at some point, but it is not always possible once they are older with families of their own, job commitments, and difficulty with traveling. This is normal and okay. I will get phone calls of well wishes and that will be wonderful.

I am used to a large grocery list of all the necessities from our traditional dinners from my childhood. This year, I have decided to spend less in order to conserve money for other needs. We will still have things like pumpkin pie and apple pie, but without the ice cream. We will have dinner rolls, cranberry sauce, corn, turkey, stuffing, gravy, and mashed potatoes. I bought most of these items a few weeks ago, when the prices were all low. It will still be lovely, even without the extras we are used to, such as cheese and crackers, fresh grapes, apple cider, nuts, chocolate cream pie, and a vegetable tray. I think, at times, we get so used to wanting an abundance of food that we may end up spending more than we can afford. This year we will have a humble Thanksgiving and we will enjoy it very much.

I remember always dressing up for dinner. We wore our nicest clothes, much like one would for the old - time Sunday Dinners after church. Thanksgiving is a wonderful holiday and a special time of giving thanks to the Lord for our blessings. I still insist the family wear their nicest clothing, and have great joy in looking our best for the occasion. I will do this, even if it is just the two of us. (But since my husband is disabled and has a great deal of physical difficulties, I may just request he wear his nicest lounging clothes!)

My mother would set the table with her best dishes. She used her nicest serving bowls and everything looked so beautiful. This was part of presenting one's best, in thanks for all we have been given. I will do this as well. I will not mind doing all the dishes. I will just take my time. We will dine with my nicest tableware, the prettiest tablecloth, and beautiful cloth napkins. I do not have a seasonal set of dishes (such as one called "Friendly Village") but someday I hope to have one added to my household. I love seeing the gorgeous table settings of others, but have accepted that it is not a practical expense for me, at this time. I love pretty things, but will happily wait, and dream, about having them someday.

Our humble table will be managed with gracious hospitality. It will be a peaceful and pleasant day. We will have prayers, and read the "Thanksgiving Proclamation" by George Washington. I have this printed out, and saved, to bring out each year. It will be a simple day of thanks and happiness.

80
Walking with a Hymn Book

I often take little walks about the house. This gives me exercise and some little diversion while being cooped up, at home, during the cold winter months. In the quiet of the day, I walk back and forth through some of the rooms. I notice the pretty curtains, the nice carpet, the landscape viewed from the windows, and the pretty Scripture verses and paintings on the walls. This gives me a sense of happiness as I walk.

Sometimes I hold a special hymn book while I walk. This book was from my Father's personal library collection that I inherited when he went home to Heaven. It is called, "*Mull's Singing Convention Number 7: Church Edition.*" It looks like it was published 20 years ago in Tennessee. It has some darling songs, which were sung by old gospel quartets. Some of the titles include: "*After Awhile*"... "*No Tears in Heaven*"... "*The Old Time Religion*" ... "*Footsteps of Jesus*" ... "*I'll Meet You in The Morning*" ... and, "*When I Wake Up to Sleep No More.*"

Several of the songs are marked, in the index, at the back of the book. These were marked by Dad, as they were some of his favorites that he knew very well.

I love singing from this treasured book while I take my daily walks. Not only do I receive the joy of physical exercise, but the blessing of spiritual exercise, from singing such precious, beloved songs. It brings such a sense of joy to my little walks about the house.

81
Lemon for your Tea

Early one morning I saw a tiny note on the parlour table by the wood stove. It was from my husband. The house was very quiet. I was the first one awake on a cold winter morning. The fire was going in the stove, and the room looked cozy by the firelight. I was very surprised to see the note. It said something like, "There are lemon wedges in the fridge for your morning tea."

I was delighted! This was going to be such a treat. I am not good at cutting lemons. My little attempts are laughable, but better than nothing. So, this was to be a great treat. I found a tiny bowl of delicate slices of lemon. I had enough lemons to last me several mornings. I found it to be such a luxury!

This has now been going on for several weeks. The bowl is frequently refilled with fresh lemon slices, as needed. I never see this happen. It is sometime, in the night, that my husband does this little kindness for me. It is a quiet work of love, which brings me great happiness.

Winter

{Photograph on Previous Page: The front grounds of Mrs. White's property.}

82
Christmas Snow Storm in Vermont

A few days ago, we had a heavy snow storm which lasted for days. Beautiful, peaceful snow fell day and night. We lost phone service the first morning. It was restored by afternoon. Next, the Internet went out. This was not working for a couple of days. We were grateful for the warmth of our cozy wood stove. We enjoyed the beautiful view out the front picture window.

Papa has already decorated the property with Christmas lights. To make me happy, one snowy evening, he turned on the lights of our outdoor Christmas tree. Then he had me go outside, with him, to see the amazing sights.

Papa brings out our Christmas tree, from his garage, every year, and sets it up out front. He built a special stand, to hold it securely in place. The very large Christmas trees, behind it, are heavy with snow. They have grown too tall for him to decorate. They make our 6 - foot tall, artificial one, look tiny by comparison!

One of the things that make me smile, are the sights of Christmas. They are so peaceful and cheerful. In the evening, as I walk in the parlour, setting things to right, Papa will say, "look outside and see your Christmas tree." This means he has turned on the lights. I love to see them!

The snow outside is thick and heavy. We have enormous snowbanks all through town. It is classic Vermont at this time of year. I hope to find a small nativity to set up on my sideboard table. I want to start getting things ready indoors for a happy Christmas season. This makes the children and grandchildren delighted with home and family. It is a special time of serving others and helping to bring happiness to those around us.

We will be singing a lot of Christmas Carols. Our favorites are "*The First Noel*" and "*Silent Night*." I want the grandchildren to learn them all, and to love them, just as we do.

This is the time to bake cookies and make fudge. This is the greatest season to practice homemaking and hospitality. We welcome guests out of the cold, winter world. We usher them in to sit by the warmth of the firelight. We offer them coffee, hot soup, and fresh bread. We give them a place to rest and to delight in the prettiness of the season.

All worries are pushed aside. We give our troubles to the Lord, in prayer, and then we go about our home-keeping. We remember to "*do all to the glory of God*." This will give us peace and joy, as it cheers the hearts of our families.

83
Mother's Homemade Birthday Tea

Last month, I invited the children and grandchildren home for a visit. I wanted to make it a special afternoon so they would have a lovely time. It gets harder to have all the family visit during Thanksgiving, and Christmas time, because some have to work, or they live a distance away. As they get older, their own family celebrations begin to form. We have to be flexible. Whenever possible, it is good to create special times to call the children home.

I thought my birthday would be a perfect excuse to have a gathering. I told the children I was going to have a tea party. Here is what I did:

I cut out several pieces of paper and placed them in a tray. These were labeled as "place- cards." As soon as the grandchildren arrived, they could take one to decorate, and write their own names. This would be a fun activity for them during the party.

I created a simple, hand - written "menu," and placed it on an empty picture holder. Here is the menu:

"Savories"
Lasagna
Cucumber sandwiches
Peanut butter and jelly sandwiches
Celery with Cream cheese and chives

"Dessert"
Mint Frosted Chocolate Cake
Cherry- Pink Frosted Chocolate Cupcakes
Chocolate Chip Cookies

"Beverages"
Tea - Sugar cubes - Lemon
Hot chocolate - Miniature Marshmallows

I had spent two days, before, making all the food, as well as cookies, cake, frosting, and cupcakes. I used a box cake recipe, and used half for a single layer cake. The other half was used for 24 mini cupcakes. I made homemade, buttercream frosting. This was from a plain recipe in an old Betty Crocker Cookbook. I divided the frosting in half so that I could create 2 different kinds:

1. Mint - I used a tiny bit of mint extract, and a drop of green food

coloring. This went on the single layer cake.

2. Cherry - I used a bit of red food coloring, to make it pink! Then I added 2 or 3 teaspoons of maraschino, cherry syrup for flavoring. This went on the miniature cupcakes.

The cookies were made from a traditional chocolate chip cookie recipe. We had a difficult time saving some for the party. We kept eating them!

I used artificial, pink and purple, flowers to decorate the sideboard table. I have had these for years already, so there was no extra cost.

I had two teapots. One was for tea, the other for hot chocolate. Years ago, one of my grown daughters had given me a Christmas teapot. This is what I used for the hot chocolate!

I mixed the cocoa in a glass measuring cup and then added some milk to cool it down. Then I poured it into the Christmas teapot. The grandchildren were delighted to be served this very special drink!

Next, they found a wonderful surprise at the tea table. I had filled the sugar bowl with miniature marshmallows! I showed the babies how to use the sugar tongs to take out one marshmallow at a time to put in their hot chocolate. One of them said, "May I have one marshmallow, Me`me?" I said, "You may have four!" They were delighted!

I served lasagna and sandwiches. I had to set up a card table, and chairs, for extra seating in our parlour. It was so nice to have everyone enjoying the food, and the fun of it all!

The grandchildren kept looking at the tiered, tea tray. They would say, "I would like a cookie next!" Or they would ask for another "bell – shaped, peanut butter sandwich." (I had used my cookie cutter when making the children's sandwiches.) Sometimes, I would see the 2-year-old looking up, dreamily, at the tiny cupcakes at the top of the display stand.

The grown-ups enjoyed all the food and service. They loved watching how much fun the children were having. It was a lovely afternoon.

Sometimes, we mothers have to "make" our own fun. We have to create homemade events to bring cheer to the family. This doesn't have to cost much, just some grocery money. We can create crafts and projects with our imagination.

Very often, children and grandchildren have no idea how to make a birthday happy for Mom or Grandma. They don't know what would make an adult happy. This is why it is often fun for all, when mother uses these times, and seasons, to serve the family by inventing a happy, homemade, celebration.

Each of the grandchildren took home their own place- card as a remembrance of the day. They were also given a lunch bag full of home-baked treats. I remember one of my girls telling me how excited her children were at the anticipation of "going to Me`me's tea party." They all had such a lovely time. I am so grateful!

84
An Evening Out

I am not used to going out in the evenings during the winter. The cold is hard to endure. I would much rather sit with some tea and stay warm by the hearth. But this month, my grandson was to be in a concert hosted by his Christian school. It was scheduled for a Thursday evening, before Christmas break. This was something I could not miss!

The week had been very busy. I was needed to babysit some of the grandchildren on different days. On two mornings, I had to get up extra early and drive into the next town to help my daughter with her four children. There were Christmas related activities going on and I was needed to help. By the afternoon before the concert, I was so exhausted I had to pray for strength. I really did not think I could manage doing one more thing. But the Lord blesses His children, and the strength came at the necessary moment!

I was babysitting my little, 16-month-old grandbaby. I had her for the afternoon and into the evening. (Normally her mother picks her up, at my house, around 8 at night.) I planned to take her with me to the concert and would bring her straight home afterwards. She is a good-natured little girl and is always smiling and happy. But carrying her and the diaper bag, in the cold, was not something I was looking forward to. It is difficult enough to get myself through a walk in the bitter, winter air. This is where I need that "will," or work ethic, and have to tell myself to "toughen up!"

I have to tell you; the entire concert was a tremendous blessing and was worth all the strength it cost me. It was just lovely. It took place at a beautiful rural church, nestled behind snow-covered trees. We had all gotten dressed up, in our best, for the evening's entertainment. Everyone looked so nice.

The students wore the traditional white top and black pants (or skirts, for girls). The grades performing were from K – 6. They did little skits, sang beautiful songs and carols, and played the most beautiful chimes and bells. I was astounded to hear hand-chimes, as the students, across the stage, were so professional and dedicated to doing their part of the program, at just the right time.

The teachers prayed and were amazingly talented in their work. I could not believe, as I sat there with little grandbaby on my lap, that this amazing school was here, in the middle of nowhere, in our rural mountain, town in Vermont.

The head of school closed the program with prayer. It felt like we had just witnessed a sort of church, on this cold winter evening before Christmas. We all left there feeling encouraged and joyful. I was so grateful to have been invited to such a wonderful program!

85
The Homemaking List

Sometimes, as I am working around the house, I like to sit at a pretty desk, or table, and write a list. It is a homemaking list. This will contain things I want to do, such as:

Bake Brownies
Tidy up the Guest Room
Write a letter
Go to the post office
Make Lasagna

It takes me several days to accomplish it all. My recent homemaking list took me 5 days to complete. Often, I will add a few more items, as I think of them. These might be fun things like:

Work on grandbaby's apron
Clear off my desk
Set a pretty table with the tablecloth and flowers
Get a package ready for the post office
Have afternoon tea with cookies

I just add things as I go along. These are not regular chores. These are just little things I like to do in my homemaking.

I once read about Jackie Kennedy's time in The White House. When she arrived, she was the mother of a little girl, and a brand-new baby. She was dedicated to her husband and children, and she also had projects she enjoyed doing. She loved antiques, and set about bringing in historical pieces as she redecorated The White House. (Each new First Lady is given a budget for redecorating.) She was also busy with social events. One day, the social secretary told her she had to do a certain task. It was something Mrs. Kennedy did not like. She was gracious in her response. Then, in her quiet and sweet demeanor, she approached the head usher in charge of the House. She confided to him in her gentle voice, "I don't **have** to do anything." That was all she had to say. Her happiness in that home was paramount.

I keep thinking about that because, for some reason, it makes me happy. We all work very hard at home. We do a great deal of work in cleaning, cooking, baking, and taking care of our families. We don't have to make homemade pizza, or coffee cake, from scratch. We don't have to bake cookies, brownies, or cake. We don't have to serve dinner at a nicely set table. The store offers many pre-made treats that can be easily obtained. There are paper plates and frozen dinners for those who want them. Yet the way in which we run our homes can bring a great deal of happiness, and comfort, to the family. Many of us do all the work because we genuinely want to.

I was just sitting here writing, while the stove bakes the brownies, and the washing machine cleans the laundry, and thinking what a blessing it is to be at home. In the middle of trials, labor, dishes, messes, and trying to keep everyone healthy and happy, we sometimes get overwhelmed and forget the quiet effort of keeping ourselves cheerful.

We should take the time to watch the sun set out the kitchen window, as we wash dishes. We could take a break, to sit out on the porch, and just enjoy the quiet afternoon air. Taking a few minutes to read a pleasant book can bring a great deal of peace and refreshment to a weary soul. These things can all be written on a list. We write them out to help us remember to take care of ourselves, as well as taking care of the family.

The homemaking list is a just bunch of thoughts we want to do to keep up our spirits. Does it make you happy to eat freshly baked brownies? I certainly enjoy them, especially if they are made from a Ghirardelli double, chocolate brownie mix! Making a batch of these will be on my list as often as possible. I also love to have Canada Dry Ginger-ale or hot chocolate. These things are luxuries to me and I write them down to remind me of lovely things that bring me joy. Writing out little notes of happy things we want to do can be a pleasant part of homemaking.

86
Confined to Home

Northern Vermont is often a sheet of solid ice, through much of the winter months. The lakes are thick, and solid enough, that many put little shacks out there, using them as camping homes, while they do their winter fishing. The driveways, walkways, and parking lots are often as icy as a skating rink.

When we first moved here, from Massachusetts, I had a great deal of trouble with the ice. I would try to open the sliding door, of our van, and, losing my footing, slam onto the ground, with an embarrassing thud. It was so sudden; it felt like I was being yanked to the ground. I would walk the pathway toward the stairs, and fall repeatedly, until I finally reached the railing, to guide me to the door. I was always slipping, and landing on my side, in parking lots. It was a common sight to see me falling, almost every single day, whenever I ventured out, in the winter months. It was painful and difficult! It was not surprising for me to be covered in bruises.

This gave me the mind-set that I would be confined to the house, during the coldest winter months. It sounded endearing. I imagined enjoying a cozy fire by the hearth while looking out, at the wintery landscape, through the window. But it never worked out that way. Someone needed me to drive somewhere, or errands had to happen. It took me a couple of years, but I finally learned how to walk on a sheet of ice. Now it is simply the bitter cold that keeps me indoors. The cold can cause one to wear out very quickly. It is an ordeal to go out into the elements, with temperatures below zero. I learned that I must wear a scarf to cover my face, from the biting winds, even on mild days.

One recent Sunday, I went out to start the car, so it would warm up before I had to leave for church. It was freezing out. The cold was so bad that the car door - lock was frozen. My key would not work. I tried over and over again and finally gave up. I was actually relieved and happy, that I could sit by the fire and read for the morning. I thought about which sermon I would listen to, on my kitchen radio. I made plans of having a little church time at home. It reminded me of the Ingalls family, from *Little House on the Prairie*. During a blizzard, or when they lived far from others, they would have church at home. That was my plan for the morning.

One of my goals has always been to never miss church. I want to go every single week. It is good for the soul. So, these rough winters are disappointing, if I have to figure it out on my own. Often, if one of my sons goes with me, or my husband is available to warm up the car for me, or shovel out the driveway, I have no trouble getting out to church. Their Yankee ingenuity, in all seasons, is a blessing! But on this particular Sunday morning, my husband was asleep. (He is disabled and often in a great deal of pain.)

Later in the morning, I was sitting by the fire reading, "*Stepping Heavenward.*" My husband woke up, and was startled to see me. "I thought you went to church?" He asked me. I told him the trouble with the frozen lock. He was soon outside to investigate.

Not long after that, he sat down beside me, on the couch, and told me a helpful lesson. "There is something on your keychain with buttons on it," he started to explain. "There is one button you push to lock the doors. There is another button to unlock the doors. The next time the lock is frozen, all you have to do is push the unlock button from the keychain." I had to smile. That was the end of my excuses, to romanticize the idea, of being confined to home, in the winter months.

87
Slow and Steady Homemaking

Home can be such a happy, restful place. It should be kept clean as much as possible. There ought to be times of washing floors, doing laundry, baking, and cooking. There are many tasks that go into keeping a nice home. These all take a great deal of effort, but they can be done with a smile, and a sense of good cheer.

To be a happy homemaker, I have learned, is to do things slowly and steadily. The other day, I was making lasagna. I am tired and sick a great deal of the time, but I try not to give - in to those obstacles. To keep my mood bright, I listen to old time gospel music on the kitchen radio. In this state of joy, I am able to do the hard labor with a good attitude. The lasagna takes me a good deal of time. I also have to clean up all the mess, and get the food baked, before the dinner hour. There are many steps and much work. I try to make this on a slower day. Washing the floors, or doing errands, should not happen when there is time consuming labor happening on the same day.

I have to keep a steady pace. I have to have times of rest. Once I get the lasagna all prepared, I will have tea and read. We need refreshment, or times of retreat, in order to keep up our energy. Then I will put the dinner in the oven. It is now time to clean the kitchen, and perhaps, listen to a comforting sermon by Charles Stanley, or another such minister, with cherished old -time values. Soon it is time to sweep the crumbs, put away laundry, and set the kitchen table. The much-anticipated rest comes, when we all get to sit at the table, and hear Papa say the prayer before the meal. Oh, how dearly much I love to sit at the dinner table, with a cloth napkin on my lap, and a beautifully set table, containing pretty dishes of homemade food. This is one of the greatest times of rest – the dinner hour!

Sometimes the phone will ring, in the early evenings, so I get to visit, as I work in the kitchen. The light of the lamps, throughout the house, adds a touch of charm, making the work more pleasant. I do the important things first – cleaning up any spills or tying up trash, so that even messes look neat. It is a slow and steady effort, which happens every single day of the year. There is no rush. There is no hurry. The work never ends. But the act of doing these precious jobs, of making a home, is a lovely part of life, at home, for Mother.

88
Well Rested

I love how children are required to have early bedtimes. They must rest each afternoon, by taking a nap, or just laying down for a time of quiet. This helps keep the children peaceful and protects their health.

I have been doing this same thing for some time now. No matter how many wonderful projects I have in mind, or how many chores I want to do, I have to stop everything for a nap. I may not always sleep during this time, but I won't allow myself to read, or do anything else. It is a time of complete rest and quiet. This protects my health and my nerves.

I am often cleaning the kitchen, or finishing up some baking, when I notice my nerves are not doing well. I can sense a feeling of stress or worry. It is similar to having anxiety. This is the time to stop and take a break. It is even better to have a normal, regular routine of stopping, at a set time each day, in order to prevent a rising surge of stress. We need times of rest every single day. I have been doing this in the early afternoons.

We had a painful day of tribulation here recently. I knew I would be needed for frequent telephone calls with extended family. I stayed in my room for most of the day, just resting with an encouraging Christian book, to provide a form of quiet, gentle recreation. (I read one of the books by Grace Livingston Hill.) I devoted all of my attention to every call that came through. Then I would pray and remember to "keep looking up." The Lord is always in control. I had to keep giving the trouble and worry to Him. Then I would go back to my book, to recover from the pain of worry and sadness.

Throughout this difficult day, I took my meals and snacks at a tray table beside my bed. I had tea and hot chocolate, and was so grateful for a time of complete rest. It was a necessary time of accomplishing nothing. I needed to be well rested to get through the ordeal. By nightfall, one last call came through. It was one of my grown daughters, with an update of temporary resolution to the trial. We could rest now. Things would be better soon. The painful crisis had passed. When she realized I had been in my room for the entire day, just feeling worn out, she said, "Stress can make us very sick, Mom. You need to try to be happy." Her encouragement gave me a sense of relief that everything was going to be okay.

Some days we may not be able to do very much. It may look like we only made the meals, or washed the dishes. It may seem like we only took care of the baby. It does not look like we are succeeding in anything.

But it is so important to have enough strength and energy, to face the work we are presented with for each day. We have to trust that God is in control, at all times. We must give Him our daily burdens. Yet, we have to always remember that trouble and trials will cause a drain on our health and happiness. It is okay to just do the very basics when this happens. Tomorrow will bring a new joy and a new strength. May we be rested, and peaceful enough, to handle it all with great faith, and a beautiful sense of grace.

89
Mottoes in a Humble Home

It was common for families to have a "Motto" to decorate the walls of their homes. This might be a painting, some hand-printed letters, or something homemade in cross stitch. Mottoes are considered "words to live by." These can be Bible verses, comforting phrases, or common wisdom.

Girls, in Colonial days, would practice their handiwork by creating mottoes out of cross stitch. I have a replica of one such piece in my home. Here is what it says:

"My Mother taught me
how to sew
And at the time
I did not know
That with every stitch
I now complete
with every row
I do so neat
My Mother's heart
is there with me
Guiding my hand for all to see
Sarah
1893"

In an old episode of *Father Knows Best,* there was a visiting salesman who asked Mrs. Anderson if she wanted to buy a "motto for her home." This was something that he had made, and framed himself, and it was inexpensive. These days, the term "motto" is not as common. But we do decorate our homes in this way, even if we just call it *wall art,* or some other modern term.

I used to hand- write out Bible verses, and do a bit of humble artwork, along with the writing. This was like a homemade motto to decorate the home.

I would just use a plain, white index card to write out the verse, such as Psalm 37:3. Then I would tape it to construction paper to create a, sort of, frame for the card. This one was placed on the wall in a child's bedroom.

We have also picked up little paintings from yard sales. These may cost as little as ten cents, or as much as a dollar. (Such as one titled, "The Difference.")

Reading these sayings is so comforting! They cheer one along the road of life!

When you enter our house, there is a door knocker that the grand-children love to use when they visit. I can hear the loud rapping on the door, and I run to let them in. Just below this door knocker is an old, beat up "Wall – Plate," inscribed with the main motto of our home, directly from Scripture. The verse is from Joshua 24:15:

". . . *as for me and my house, we will serve the Lord.*" {The wall - plate, for those who are long -time readers, was something I bought early in my marriage, at a tiny Christian store. It has been with us for nearly three decades, and has been in every apartment, or home, we have lived in. It had been lost for a few years, but was recently found, and restored to its rightful place.}

There are both humble mottoes and newer ones in our home. One of my favorites contains the hymn, "*Amazing Grace*" with a beautiful painting above it.

I originally saw the *Amazing Grace* painting in a flower shop of a funeral home in rural Alabama. It was a sad time, but I was so cheered by this painting. In every funeral of my family, the service closes with everyone singing, "*Amazing Grace*." Shortly after seeing this, I came across a small version, in a gallery's bankruptcy sale, in the lobby of a rural mall. I was so happy to buy it, at a fraction of its

Homemaking for Happiness

cost. It inspires my faith and comforts me, every time I look at it.

We also have magnets that cheer us along. One has a beautiful lighthouse, with an ocean scene, and is paired with a comforting Scripture verse from Psalm 27:1.

On the wall of my bedroom is a beautiful painting that brings me great peace. It is a midnight blue, in color, with a cowboy on a horse. He is holding a lantern, and a little lamb that he is bringing to safety. There is a Bible verse written out, from Isaiah 46:4. I had originally bought this painting for my mother, right after she became a widow. Dad was her cowboy, her protector. This beautiful picture brought her great comfort and peace. Now that Mother has gone home to Heaven, to be with Dad, this painting is in my room, to remind me of the precious promise of our Lord.

There are difficult days when we all get very anxious and worried. This is especially true when we are worried about the trials and troubles of teenagers and grown children. A very dear lady made a framed gift for me: She did a cross stitch of Philippians 4: 6 – 7, and her husband made the frame. This is a precious gift that really brings me a great deal of peace. When I start to worry, I just read this, and I give all my burdens and worries to the Lord.

We have a lovely painting right in our parlour, above the coat rack. We found it at a yard sale, many years ago. It is so pretty and contains a floral scene and, "The Lord's Prayer."

It is lovely to have pretty things to look at throughout the home. The sayings bring us comfort, remind us of our focus, and encourage us. Anyone who enters our home knows what our motto is!

I came across some photographs from the Library of Congress. A Photographer, from the U.S. Farm Administration, visited a family and took some pictures in 1943. There is one of a young boy, sitting near a Motto, on the wall, of his Washington D.C. home. It says, "Jesus Never Fails."

There is another picture, to go with this one, of this same young boy, with his mother in their kitchen. It says they are home after church. It is an old- time Christian family, like many of us, even today.

A humble home is a place where materialism is not the focus. It is a place of rest and old-time values. It is where the simple life originates. Filling our surroundings with old- time mottoes of comfort, and encouragement, is a precious way to build our courage and faith. It will bring a smile of cheer, and a nod of contented peace.

90
Church Clothes

It used to be common for children to have at least one nice outfit for church. A good suit for boys and a pretty dress for girls were simply called, "Church clothes." Most often, a new outfit was purchased to coincide with the yearly Easter Sunday service. The nicest dresses are usually available, in abundance, at all the stores just when spring arrives.

This type of purchase could be planned to happen once each year. Careful shopping at store sales can make this affordable. When money is very difficult, there are thrift stores to frequent until just the right garments are found, at a very low cost.

We girls always had a few special dresses that were good for church, and any special occasion. The boys had one good suit. I have tried to do this with my own five children, as they were growing up. It is so important for each of us, especially children and young adults, to have at least one outfit suitable for church. There is something so charming to see little ones in respectful clothing, that bring out the reverence and dignity in us all.

91
Diary of a Clean House

I have been cleaning so much the last few days, it has been fun! I wanted to share some ideas with you on how to keep a beautifully, clean house, even in a humble environment. This work of cleaning has an incredible side benefit. It provides you with good health. I will share a diary of the work I have been doing, along with some suggestions for your own home:

Sweeping and Washing Floors

1. Last week, I started a new habit of sweeping and washing the bathroom and kitchen floors each Monday morning. I do this before anyone else wakes up. The house is quiet and the work goes quickly.

Since I have been doing it at about the same time each week, I have become more efficient, and the work goes fast. It takes me about 20 minutes, including moving things out of the way (such as small carpets, kitchen stools, trash barrels, toy baskets, etc.).

I thought that would be enough exercise for me for the day, so I planned to skip my normal workout. But after I finished the floors, I thought it would be relaxing to go walk on the treadmill, while the floors dried.

I listen to the *Old Fashioned Revival Hour* program while I walk. It includes singing from the congregation, choir, and a quartet. It also has a brief sermon. I find it refreshing to hear the program while I exercise.

By the time I was finished, the floors were all dried and looked wonderful. I put everything back in its place. The little plum - colored carpet went back on the floor, in front of the kitchen sink. The stools were back by the counter. The grandchildren's toy baskets were placed back under the sideboard table, and all was neat again.

The second week I did this, everything was much easier. I had a routine in place. I knew what it would cost me, in strength and time, to do all the work. I also became more efficient because, as we all know, the more you do something, the more skilled you become.

Rest

2. It was time to rest and have some refreshment. I had tea and a homemade muffin. After doing all that exercising and work, it was important to take a break. I also read a book for a little while.

When we start feeling better, it is time to get back up and do some more work. The labor of housekeeping keeps us productive, makes our home look nice, and keeps us active.

Kitchen Work

3. I made a batch of homemade pizza. Company arrived and I had to feed them a nice lunch. While I did the work, I made several little pizzas for the freezer. I cleaned the kitchen while we all visited. I had four of my little grandchildren here, and there were plenty of dishes to do. They enjoyed apple juice, pizza, and some muffins while they were here. They also colored and used play-dough at the table.

I have to tell you that I was surprised that I had any energy left, after such a busy morning! But truthfully, all this work (combined with good nutrition and necessary rest) keeps us healthy.

Another Break and Thoughts on Health

4. It was time to stop and rest again. This is a good time for me to explain the amazing health benefit of cleaning and exercising. My mother had diabetes. She was not an active person, because she had a very social personality. Everywhere she went, she would stop to talk to everyone. She would stand in grocery store lines and visit with the other customers. She would sit at Ladies Bible study meetings and just talk and visit. At home, she was often sitting and talking to us, or talking on the phone. Everyone loved her, but this did not provide her much opportunity to be physically active. She would have to force herself to stop everything and just walk. This helped regulate her blood sugar levels. Mom was also an excellent

housekeeper. She often cleaned throughout the day. This was another way to regulate her blood sugar levels. She never thought about this, it was just a benefit of her keeping busy.

I have the opposite problem. I have hypoglycemia. I have always had this. I would need to eat frequent, small meals to regulate my sugar levels. However, I notice that when I am cleaning or exercising, or just going out on errands, and keeping busy in the physical sense, I do not need to eat all the time. I feel fine!

So when we are resting too much, or watching television too much, or reading too long, we often want to keep having snacks or meals! We eat far more food, and much more often, when we are not physically busy.

Keeping busy will maintain your weight and your good health. Cleaning the house is going to provide you with more energy than you ever imagined!

Have you ever felt like you were too sick or too tired to do anything? Try cleaning for 15 minutes and you will notice a great improvement! You will feel better.

Doing the Laundry

5. I recently got so tired (and lazy) that I did not bother to fold or put away the laundry after the dryer stopped. I just piled it all in the basket. All of a sudden, I had to iron our clothes for church on Sunday. I had to iron many things over the next few days. All this because of one day, when I did not bother to take the time to put away our laundry.

This week, I listened for the dryer and got right up and took care of it all. It saved me a great deal of time, and worry, by just doing it right away instead of putting it off.

Dusting and Vacuuming

6. It took me 15 minutes to dust and vacuum the upstairs rooms. I used a pink, feather duster for some of the furniture. Then I used furniture polish, with a rag, for the end-table and hutch. I loved taking down some family photographs, and pretty things, to dust and take care of them.

I have some very old, worn -out furniture. There are scuffs, and chips, and scrapes over some of it. But with a good dusting, our humble belongings looked fresh, bright, shiny, and neat!

It is amazing how powerful modern vacuum cleaners are. If you have a good one, it doesn't take long to simply go over the carpets and make the rooms look nice.

Washing Windows and Mirrors

7. It is hard to keep windows clean in winter. I can wash them from the inside only. But someone will need to get on a ladder, to do the glass on the other side, for most of the house. Regardless of the trouble, it is still important to get a glass cleaner and wipe down those windows. This does not take long at all. I quickly cleaned all the mirrors. I just use a store brand glass cleaner and a cleaning rag.

Everything looked fresh and smelled clean.

More Company

8. Before the day was over, I had some company drop by. I did a little crocheting as we visited. This was a wonderful opportunity for me to take some time for a little bit of rest. It is refreshing to visit, and just be happy, in the fellowship of others.

Cleaning the Stairs

9. After the company left, I had a brownie and some ginger-ale. I thought I had better do another chore to work off that treat! I gathered together a scrub brush and a bucket of hot, soapy water and went to clean the wooden staircase, which goes to our third floor. I cleaned each step, and the sides of the wall, all the way up. I did this slowly and used an old towel, to dry each one, as I finished. This was hard and time-consuming work. When I was halfway finished, I felt very tired. But I kept going. I had a goal to do this work, and I wanted to finish the job. But by the last two steps I felt weary. There is a big difference between feeling tired and being genuinely weary. We will always be tired. That is life. But when you are weary, it is time to stop. That was the last chore I did for the day. My work was done.

Little Jobs of Housekeeping

10. Throughout the day, I will dust light fixtures, wipe down light switches, or sweep the entryway. These little jobs of cleaning the house are often done at odd times, in the middle of simply living life.

Have you ever noticed your front entry, and thought it would be good to just sweep and wash it really quick? Or maybe you notice a bit of dust accumulating on picture frames. These tiny jobs take mere minutes and can be done whenever you feel discouraged by sitting still for too long.

We can live our lives, doing projects, taking care of the family, and doing all the basics of home-keeping. In the midst of all this, it is wonderful to just get up and do some little bit of cleaning to brighten the home. You will find your strength, and energy, soar as your house becomes neat and pretty!

More Rest Than Work

11. I have to add one more note to this. We are all going to have our good and bad days. We may be in pain, or terribly ill. We may be stressed, or have things come up, that interfere with our ability to clean. That is normal life. I am not trying to run a marathon here. None of us need to try to win, or be the best at housekeeping. We need peace. We need contentment. We need to enjoy our days. Mothers need to have more periods of rest, and refreshment, than labor. This is important to keep us gentle and sweet.

I want to be rested enough to sit on the couch and read stories to grandbabies. I cannot wear myself out so much, from hard work, that I am useless. The point of encouraging each other to clean our houses is to make the most of our time. It is to find all those spare moments to do the little jobs which will make our homes pleasant, while strengthening our health at the same time. This is something we can all do, even if we only begin with *a few minutes* of effort.

92
Proper Speaking

I have noticed a little trouble in my conversation with the family. When I am sitting at the table with the grandchildren, they will request some activity, or treat, while their Mother is not present. I tell them, "You will have to ask your mother." But they sometimes pause and look at me a little puzzled. I have come to realize that I talk too fast, with a strong Boston accent frequently emerging, if I am not careful. This is difficult for the children to comprehend. All of the grandbabies were born here in Vermont. I do not detect an accent in this region. It is mostly common English, other than from those who are from the old-time farms. This means we are all surrounded by normal, carefully spoken English.

My accent comes from having grown up in a suburb of Boston. I was raised in a Massachusetts family, who go back a few generations in the same town. Some of our relatives commuted to the city of Boston for college or jobs. Their accents were quite thick. I have just always assumed everyone could understand what we were saying.

So, when the babies ask my permission, and get my response of "You will have to ask your mother," they are really hearing (said very briskly), "Yuh hafta ask yuh muthah." I am learning to slow down, and carefully enunciate my words.

This reminds me of when my youngest was being homeschooled. We moved here to Vermont when he was only 5 - years old. By the time he was in his pre-teen years, we noticed a barrier in our communication. I would give him a spelling test. He had to frequently stop me, and explain that my accent was making it difficult for him to understand the words I wanted him to spell! I had to exaggerate the words and speak very slowly, because it was difficult for me to re-train my way of speaking.

Now, with the grandchildren, I am seeing that I must work harder in my words. I do, however, notice many sweet things about their precious baby talk. They will shout out, "juice!" I will look at them and say, "How nice. Juice is nice." I want them to come right out and ask me for a drink, using a full sentence. So, I say to them, "Me`me, may I have some juice please?" They will repeat this, and are rewarded with the requested beverage. We have fun with our language.

I think what is sweetest of all, is hearing the 2 year – old, from his highchair. Since he is the youngest of four children, he has an incredible grasp of vocabulary. He also repeats many words he hears his own mother say. This can be greatly amusing to us all, especially the other day when I went to pick him up out of his seat. He quickly grabbed his cup and said, "I want my juice, actually." His mother smiled and said he just started saying "actually" all the time. We cannot help but laugh, at all the fun and mishaps we have, as we attempt to properly speak in our home.

Of course, none of us want to lose the beautiful heritage of our way of talking. I love to hear the chatter of my family, back home in Massachusetts. It is a comforting sound of a true Boston accent. These are charming little differences that make life so interesting. We just have to learn how to communicate in a way that the next generation can understand.

93
The Benefit of Staying Home

Last spring and summer, I was frequently travelling with my oldest daughter and her two little boys. We were always going somewhere for appointments, errands, and visits. It was a very busy season that kept me away from home a great deal. Now that the cold months of winter have arrived, I am staying home most of the time.

My days are very slow – paced and calm. There is no rush or hurry. There is little stress. This is the greatest benefit of staying home. I am able to exercise, in the early morning hours, just as the sun is rising. Then I will bake and do a little cleaning.

I have been re-reading many of the Grace Livingston Hill books. I love her description of homemaking and living a godly life. Her stories are also fascinating and entertaining. Then I take a break, from this time of recreation, and do some "work."

So far, I have been able to hand-sew the hems of a half dozen cloth napkins I made. I have several more to keep me occupied. I enjoy setting up the ironing board, and pressing the fabric, before pinning the hems in place. Then I set the fabric aside for when I have time to do the hand - work. I usually sew while I am on the phone, or when I am sitting with the family in the parlour.

I have crochet projects and writing projects I can do as time allows. I am making simple dresses for the upcoming warm weather. I have flowery fabric for homemade pillowcases I will make, to brighten up sofas and chairs throughout the house. I also have plenty of time to organize rooms and get an early start on spring cleaning. It is the season of indoor work, while the outside world is very cold and quiet, here in northern New England.

The dishes are done after each meal or snack. The floor is kept swept and tidy. I do the laundry and put out fresh towels each day. I keep the home ready for our frequent visitors. Grown children and grandchildren come by, several times, each week. I am here for whenever I am needed, both at home, and on the telephone. I am not rushed or worn down. This is the joy and reward of being a homemaker.

Our little home is a haven of rest. I am able to cultivate this precious place, of peace and happiness, because I have very little outside cares at this time. I am able to stop whatever I am doing, at any time, to read to one of the babies. The babies come alongside me and help in my work. I teach them to say their prayers, and delight in hearing their little voices thanking the Lord for their food and snacks.

I have learned to shut out the worry of the world's news, which has become a constant source of anxiety for us all. My parents used to watch the 6:00 news when I was a child. There were the local and international stories, and the weather, which interested us all. It took no longer than 30 minutes a day. Then we went back to the cares of our own family, and home life. I am trying to recreate this, here, in our quiet little, rural home. I will not allow the stress of the world to overtake the peace of our home.

The days, and years, go by so quickly. To stay home, focus on home, and to create a family-centered life, takes a great deal of unhurried time. While we all can choose to do a great many things, and be pulled away for so many worthy causes, the greatest need, in our day, is for Mothers to just be home.

94
Playing the Food Game

I love reading restaurant menus. The list of food available in a breakfast buffet, or dinner menu, is always inviting. The way they describe the dishes make it all sound amazing. We love to talk about food around here. Someone will say, "Wouldn't it be nice to have an ice cream sundae?" Or someone will dream about a delicious Italian dinner, with fresh baked bread and butter. I call this "playing the food game." We are talking about things we either, do not have, or wish we could enjoy. My husband had some dental work recently and could not eat very much. He started the game one evening.

He talked about a restaurant buffet and we each took turns pretending to pick out whatever food we wanted. His first selection was for breakfast. He wanted *two* orders of eggs, hash brown potatoes, toast, and coffee. He has a large appetite! Then it was my turn. I wanted little, silver dollar pancakes from the children's menu. He laughed because my portions of food are always so much smaller than his. Then we chose dessert items, selected lunch entrees, and smiled over what we both wanted for dinner. As we talked, I thought how wonderful it would be if I could jot down everything we said. It would be a fun, and easy way, to create menu ideas for the coming week.

95
The Day I Did Not Meet Franklin Graham

I have wanted to take a trip to visit the Billy Graham library and Museum. I have been talking about this dream, to Papa, for years. He will say, "Someday, I will take you there." We talk about how long the drive is to North Carolina from here in Vermont. We would need to stop at hotels, pay for gas, buy food, and take several days. It sounded expensive. My husband is not able to travel by airplane because of his disability. But the drive in the car, for such a long trip, will cause too much pain, without frequent stops and overnight rest. This is why, to this date, the trip remains only a distant dream.

This month, it came to my attention that Franklin Graham was doing an event, right here in my state. It was the, "Decision America – Northeast Tour," and Vermont was the first stop! Our winter weather had been mild enough for a few days, to give me enough confidence to travel. After much discussion, among the family, it was decided that I could attend. The tickets were free and easily obtained. I was delighted! My 21 – year old son was to go with me. The drive to the city, where the event was to be hosted, would take 2 hours. We were going to wear our best church clothes.

Franklin was to speak at a conference center in one of the city hotels. Guests were to enjoy refreshments and good Christian fellowship. Mr. Graham was to give a message on bringing the gospel to those in our own communities. It would be a training session that we dearly needed to hear.

Early on the morning of our trip, I looked out the window. The wind was fiercely raging. A blizzard had hit our area. The constant snowfall, and blowing wind, made visibility impossible. I knew, in that very moment, that I could not go. I watched the storm throughout the morning, with a wistfulness of yielded resignation. *Not my will*, I thought, *but Thine*.

Shortly after Papa woke up, and assessed the situation, he asked me to sit down for a minute. "Could I talk to you?" he asked in a gentle voice. I smiled weakly and said, "I know. I can't go." He wanted to break the news to me in such a caring way. But I already knew I would not get to meet Franklin Graham that day. I would stay home and be happy, just as I have done for many years. I am grateful, so grateful, for my home and family. I accept, and understand, that visiting the Billy Graham museum is only a dream. But someday, for sure and for certain, I will meet him and all the wonderful Christian workers, over on the other shore – when we all meet in Heaven.

96
Focus on the Home

A Mother's job is to keep her home as happy and pleasant as she possibly can. There is plenty of cooking, cleaning, planning, and mending to do. In the midst of all this duty, she can have a cheerful, servant's heart. Being productive, and doing one's very best, gives us a sense of peace and happiness.

Sometimes, the world's trouble enters the parlour and causes disruption, stress, and even fear. We have to keep fighting off this kind of invasion. This may be by limiting access to the newspapers, the television news, and even the constant stream of internet reports on the misery around us. While we should certainly care and pray, we cannot take our focus away from the home.

What I see before me, is my house, my family, my local church, and my own community. This is where I am called to be. This is my very own mission work. We cannot take on the burdens of the entire world. We must do the work before us.

I try to tell others that I don't want to hear about all the bad things going on. I know what the un-churched world is like. I cannot handle the constant updates. But I am available for a "call to action." This happened recently. I had to call my local representative, at the State House, and ask them to vote "no" on a terrible bill that I was against. Then I put this into God's hands and left the burden there. I went back to my work of making a home.

While so much of this chaos rages outside my door, some of my grandchildren will stop by, with their Mother, for a visit. This is the essence of life – the family. This is what brings me joy. I focus on the children. Little 4-year-old grand-girl always brings a bag from home. She packs a toy, a little blanket, and a pair of slippers. She wants to be comfortable and cozy at Me`me's house. (When I visit her, I also bring slippers and a housecoat.) The children all smile as they enter my house. They are all bundled up in winter coats and hats. My 6 – year- old grandson asked for my Bible. He wanted to read us some of what he is learning in the Christian school. He was so happy to open up the Bible and tell us how much he loves it. What a blessing! It is so much easier to focus on a happy home, when there are precious little ones who need us to be cheerful.

Papa and I will daily sing hymns, pray together, and read the Bible, in the evening. We do the religious duties that bring us incredible peace and contentment. We keep doing God's work no matter what is happening in the world around us.

We have to always remember - the calamity outside the door will always be going on. But our little homes are lighthouses of holiness where we, despite our own flaws, do our very best to bring happiness and godliness to our families and neighborhoods. This is why we cannot let the news destroy our peace. We know the world is at enmity with God. This is nothing new. This is no surprise to us. We are not of the world. We must stand straight and tall, and do the precious work of keeping cheerful homes for the Lord. It is desperately needed, in all times, and in all places, throughout the ages. This is the greatest work a Mother can do. . . Focus on the Home.

97
Christmas Tea Party

I wanted to have a special event to delight some our grandchildren, who live nearby. I made plans with one of my daughters to have her family over one weekday morning. She brought along her five little children. These are the grandchildren that I am helping to homeschool this year. I told them we would have a Christmas tea party.

As the day for the event approached, the children were very excited. They could not wait to go to Me`me's house for the tea party.

I set the table with my best tea pot. It has a Christmas design and looks festive. I filled this up with hot chocolate for the children to enjoy. I use my sugar dish for miniature marshmallows. A set of silver tongs sits beside this bowl, to make things fun. I filled up a little creamer cup with cold milk from the refrigerator. The table was all set and pretty when the children arrived.

To bring an extra sense of happiness, I set out all my winter village houses on the sideboard table. These plug in and can be turned on to light up the windows of the little houses and shops. I have a lace doily placed in front, with a tiny snowman figurine, in front of the village. To the left is a pretty hot chocolate store with figures standing beside it, enjoying a happy winter day. The children stood staring at the scene with a quiet sense of wonder. It added to the excitement of the day.

The children had a lovely time watching me pour out each cup of hot chocolate from the pretty tea pot. I went through the entire, formal routine of pouring a bit of milk, from the creamer, into each cup. Then each child took a turn, using the silver tongs, to help themselves to a few miniature marshmallows to add to their drinks.

I served cheese and crackers and a little fruit. I made miniature chocolate cupcakes, with silver foiled lining, and topped them with strawberry frosting. These looked wonderful on each child's plate. It was a wonderful treat for all of us.

Each child was given a little gift and then it was time to go downstairs to play. Papa had set up our train set, on a card table, by the picture window. When the children entered that room, they were surprised and happy. The train went around the track and made charming sounds of a real train. We had such fun just watching, and listening, as it went on its little route around the circle.

I handed out tiny books of Christmas carols to each of the children. We sang the old favorites including, "*Silent Night*" and, "*Hark the Herald Angels Sing.*" The younger children tried to follow along in their books, even though they were not yet ready to read.

The children were all dressed up in their nicest Church clothes. The youngest, a baby of just a few months old, brought such joy to the celebration. I sent the children home with a bag full of extra cupcakes and other treats. They had their gifts, under their arms, after they put on their warm winter coats and gloves. It was time to trudge out into the snowy day and head back home. It had been a wonderful Christmas visit.

98
Strength to do What is Right

Have you ever wondered why some people have a lot of self-discipline? They do not overeat. They will not eat junk food. They do their work on time. They exercise regularly. They are genuinely good people. I think this has a lot to do with learning from one's mistakes. It means that they have suffered the consequences of wrong behavior and do not want to suffer again. This builds up their will to do what is right.

We learn these lessons through our mistakes and through the guidance of the Lord. This self-discipline can extend to many good things in our lives. For example: We do not want the consequences of a messy house, so we clean it daily. We do not want to get sick, by eating a bunch of candy, so we avoid it. It affects our health and our surroundings. It is an important quality to cultivate. It is learning to avoid sin and destruction, and instead, seeking the good and the blessings.

We need self-discipline, but it takes a great deal of energy. The culture around us seeks ease, luxury, and pampering. It seeks laziness. There is hard work involved in doing difficult things. It takes practice and pep talks and time. Where do we get the strength, for instance, to do the dishes after a long day of hard work? We get it from a sense of duty. It is a discipline of life to do what is right and good. This sense of duty gets stronger every time we keep doing the work. This is self-discipline, which comes from daily serving the Lord. Every time you do the right thing, you will build strength of character and a strong sense of duty. This is a blessing!

99
Detached from Technology

I had gotten into the habit of checking my computer every time I wanted to know the day's weather report. It seemed like I needed the exact temperature several times a day. This information was then announced throughout the house. I was giving the family constant, unsolicited, updates.

I finally realized how much time and effort I was wasting. This was a modern pastime. In my childhood home, we had an outdoor thermometer attached to our side porch. It was rarely even used. We were perfectly capable of stepping outside, or opening a window, to find out the weather. There was also an evening weather report, on television, to help us plan our activities, and choice of clothing, for the coming days.

These days, it is too easy to constantly lean on technology for things that do not matter. We will be in a constant battle to avoid the temptation of wasting time on idle concerns. In my free time, I would rather sit and mend, visit with the family, read a book, or take a quiet walk outdoors. I am learning to detach myself from the need of too much technology. This will provide a peaceful life, with pleasant thoughts, and time for what matters.

100
Reading Through the Bible with Mister

Last month, my husband and I finished reading through the entire Bible together. This was the first time my husband had read, or heard, the entire Bible. It took us four and a half years. It was such an incredible blessing to have this precious time of Bible reading, each night, for such a long period of time.

We started doing this shortly after his injury. He had been in a frightening accident that caused permanent damage, and his permanent disability. We spent a great deal of time going to physical therapists, seeing specialists, and attending many doctor appointments. One night I offered to read the Bible to him. I read a short chapter in Psalms. We did this again the following night. Soon I was saying a short prayer after the reading. Then I asked if we could sing a hymn from one of our hymn books. He agreed.

Eventually, my husband was the one saying the prayers. Soon he was picking out his own Bible passages to read to me. Then he selected 1 to 4 hymns, each night, and we sang together.

Over a period of several months, we established a precious routine of Bible time, which went like this:

1. I read, out loud to him, one to two chapters in the Bible (with the intention of reading through the entire Book to him.)
2. He read a chapter, out loud, that he had selected from the Psalms.
3. We sang hymns from our hymn books.
4. Later, at the end of the day, he said a prayer, out loud - every single night.

If any of our grown children happened to be visiting with us, at the time of our evening devotions, they would sit with us and listen, or join in the singing.

There were some difficult days when I had to be away from home. (This would be for an overnight trip to stay with one of our grown children.) I would call my husband on the telephone, at the appointed time, and he would read a Psalm to me over the phone. Then he would pray. It was so comforting.

A few months after we established our Bible routine, I would have a prayer request before the evening prayer. I would say, "One of the grandbabies has a cold." Or, "I am not feeling well." Or, "I am scared or worried." He would include this concern in his prayers. The Lord heard our prayers and our faith grew stronger.

In all of the four and a half years, of doing our evening Bible time, we only missed one night. This was because I was having a rough day. I was not in a good mood. I let this ruin my day. I said to my husband, "I do not want to do Bible time tonight. I am going to bed."

Then I cried myself to sleep because I was so miserable, feeling like I was missing out on our beloved time of Bible reading. I felt terrible. From this, I learned to keep my moods in check, and get over a bad mood quickly, so I would never miss our evening devotions again. It was a difficult lesson, but one I learned very quickly.

On other nights, I would be very sick in bed. I could not sing or talk without coughing. On those nights, my husband would sit in the rocking chair beside my bed. He would read a chapter to me from his Bible. Then he would sing a verse, or two, of one of our favorite hymns. We were determined never to miss a night of Bible reading, even if one of us was sick.

There were times when the days had been stressful and the hour would get late. On these days we would simply read something like Psalm 23 and then sing one hymn. On better nights, I would read several chapters in Psalms, or nearly all of the book of Esther or Ruth - in one sitting. But our usual routine was for me to read 2 chapters, in order, to accomplish our goal of reading through the Bible. Then my husband would always select a Psalm to read to me. After this, he would pick out four hymns.

When we started doing this, my husband did not know that many hymns. He was familiar with "*Amazing Grace,*" but not much more than that. Every now and then, I would suggest a new one, and sing it for him. He learned many hymns in this way, and found many favorites. He marked the ones we know in his own hymn book. He now has 23 hymns marked in his book. He has memorized every single one of these.

Sometimes, as we go about our day, in different rooms of this old house, I can hear my husband singing one of the hymns as he goes about his chores. I am so grateful and blessed to hear this.

His faith and wisdom have grown tremendously over the last four years. There were times I felt troubled about some trial or difficulty. My husband was able to direct me to the Lord, with a reminder of something we had read in the Bible. Or, he would mention a verse from one of the hymns. This would give me courage and peace!

Last month, after we finished reading the entire Bible, we started again in Genesis. Our goal is to read the entire Bible in about 2 years. But there is no rush. The purpose is not to have pressure or meet an unrealistic goal. We may not make it within the 2 years. But we will continue on, night after night, year after year, to the best of our ability; Even if we have many nights of only reading a chapter in Psalms.

101
The Noon Meal

I have been reading about how old-time families would gather together, each day, for the noon meal. This was their dinner time. If children were in a local school, they would come home for their lunch break. Dad would be working in town, or in the fields of his farm, and would pause to go home to eat a meal, at the kitchen table, with his family.

Isn't it nice to imagine a hot lunch of home cooked goodness that Mom makes herself? There may have been bread, milk, meat, and some fresh or canned vegetables from the garden. This was the time to nourish the family with comforting food from home. Dad would say a precious prayer to ask the Lord's blessing on the food.

Dad would have a little coffee while the family visited together and talked about their day. It was a nice, happy rest, from the labor of the morning.

The children would laugh and enjoy the time of fellowship with their brothers and sisters. They would enjoy sitting near Mother and Dad, finding security and happiness in the routine and tradition of the dinner hour.

This was the leisure hour before heading back to work, or school, for the rest of the afternoon. It helped to bond the family.

These days, I think the practice, here in the United States of America, has slipped away. It is no longer convenient to join together for the noon meal. It is not practical in many cases. It is more common for us to have the supper hour together.

We can revive the tradition of the noon meal each evening. Mother can make a hot meal and set a pretty table. This is the place where we learn our manners as we display kindness and courtesy. This is the time to bond together, enjoying a rest, as we eat Mother's home cooking.

After the meal, it may be common for the children to wash up all the dishes, and help mother clean the kitchen. Then the family might sit together to read, play the piano, sing hymns, or just enjoy some home projects in the living room.

Home is the greatest institution on earth. It ought to be a peaceful place of compassion, patience, and love. Meal times provide a great opportunity to spend time together at the old kitchen table. These will give us many happy memories of home, Mother and Dad, and pleasant childhood days.

102
Go on Sowing

We, as children of the dear Lord, are grateful to do His work. We read our Bibles, listen to precious sermons, and pray heartfelt – earnest prayers. We want the light of holiness, peace, and joy to shine through our lives. But the work is hard.

I see so much brokenness around me. People dearly need the beautiful message of the Word of God. They need the comfort of Scriptures. They need the courage in knowing that the Lord walks alongside us, on these many difficult roads.

We need to be the example of walking this life, with great patience and incredible integrity, that only comes from a closeness with the Lord.

So many times, we do our work, we do the labor, and yet, we see no results. We do the precious work and we are discouraged when there is no improvement in the lives and hearts of others. They may be sad, hurting, in pain, or suffering. We have to keep sowing, keep doing the cherished work of living with grace, mercy, kindness, forgiveness, and understanding, with a sense of beloved virtue. We are grateful to serve without murmuring, because we love Him. They will see this and wonder.

Sometimes we will see glimmers of joy, and rejoice in treasured victories! At other times, we may only see long roads of hard toiling. But we must go on sowing. The Lord will bless the harvest, even if we are not able to see the result. We must trust Him with our very lives. This gives us the faith to toil on. He is the one who will bring forth changed lives, and reconciliations, with the peace that passeth all understanding.

103
Keeper of the House

I have not been able to do as much housework as I would like. I want to keep the house and be a good homemaker. But time and energy are limited. The rooms are neat, but the vacuuming and the floor washing have been neglected. I am grateful to at least accomplish one or two important matters each day.

In the midst of all the work, and worries from the world around us, I like to do a little neat decorating that brings happiness to us all. I try to do these no matter how tired I get. Have you ever looked at the kitchen table and thought it would be nice to put out a fresh tablecloth? But that extra bit of energy takes a great deal of effort! In most cases, I would do it anyway. It doesn't take long to make things look cheerful. Perhaps it is only 10 minutes of effort, here and there, throughout the day, to add that extra touch of happiness in homemaking.

Every house needs a keeper. Someone has to do that little work to keep things clean and pleasant. Someone has to do the shopping, plan the meals, do the laundry, make the beds, and keep things nice. It is such an honor and a privilege to be the keeper of the house.

Whenever I have some especially difficult work to do, I find a nice old-fashioned sermon to play on the kitchen radio. It is easier to work when hearing a precious message. Today, I heard Dr. Harold Sightler preach, "*What Are They Among So Many*?" I believe he was around 80 years old at the time of this sermon. It is powerful and encouraging. This helped strengthen me to do the work of making a homemade batch of pizza for the freezer. I always keep out a few of the pizzas, for the day's lunch, when I make this. I love to hear old fashioned sermons, and old gospel music, as I work. It brings me a sense of peace and joy.

We had a great deal of snow today. The roads are quiet and peaceful. There are no crowds in our rural, mountain village. The wood pellet stove is keeping the parlour cozy. One would not even imagine there is trouble in the world, by just enjoying the happiness of home life. This is what I hope to provide for all my family and guests - a place of refuge!

The little duties of keeping house are what keep our minds busy. The morning work of making beds, sweeping the kitchen floor, and cleaning the breakfast dishes, can bring peace, if we remember to do it all for God's glory. We do our work for the dear Lord. We trust Him for all things. Remembering this, as we work, creates a precious bond, in our hearts, to our Father in Heaven.

Nothing needs to be done in a hurry, for that would only cause stress and panic. Why should we worry? It is better to schedule the chores, throughout the day, in order to do it calmly. We must not let the problems, of the outside world, affect our mood. If mother is calm and cheerful, in her work, the entire household will benefit.

104
Clothing Allowance

In modern budgets, there is a spending category for clothing. The amount varies in different households, but many consider this to be a necessity. I have often been amazed that budgets include an allowance for clothing, every single month of the year. I have heard some say they spend $100 each month on clothes. Others spend $50. Some even spend $30 or more, every week, on clothing. They may buy things during casual visits to department stores or thrift shops. These may not be planned, but just done on an impulse. This is what I think of when I hear the term, "clothing allowance."

I am not personally familiar with this type of spending. We have never had a clothing allowance. My parents bought us seasonal items that were necessary. We would look through our current wardrobe, discarding what no longer fit. A list of items would be made and then we would buy those items at two specific times during the year. This would happen just before fall. Another small trip was made just before summer. Then at Christmas time, we were given pajamas, or some clothing, as gifts. Each spring, just before Easter, we would get a new church outfit.

I have done similar clothing shopping for my own children and grandchildren. Often it takes time for us to save up enough money for the trip to the store. We then spend only the amount of money that we have available in cash.

I have gone some years without buying any clothing. I have experienced a clothing shortage, where I have worn clothes for such a long time, that the fabric was fading so much, there would be holes in places. I would do my best to mend, and repair, to make the clothes last as long as possible. These things happen during difficult financial times. We make do, and get by, when there is little money.

While clothing is a necessity, it is not something that needs to be purchased very often, particularly for adults. When times get better, we can get back to the seasonal shopping, replacing items that are well worn.

I do not buy clothes based on changing fashions. I buy classic items that will last long and wear well. This saves a great deal of money, and prevents a great deal of waste.

Since I have gone years without the ability to buy anything, I am not inclined to simplify my closet. I keep a variety of clothing, that I have accumulated over many years. In this way, I have church clothes, nightgowns, house robes, casual dresses and skirts, and seasonal, comfortable tops. I know what it is like to go without. I will not discard perfectly good clothing, because I never know when a financial crisis will happen, causing me to go without decent clothes again for years.

I believe we ought to look our very best. It is a blessing to look nice and to dress nicely. This helps bring beauty and cheer, to ourselves, and to those around us. We can carefully plan to buy a lovely wardrobe at a reasonable price. The amount is based on our personal finances. It is based on how much we can afford, without going into debt, or affecting the ability to pay our basic bills.

Since I have never had a clothing allowance (money given regularly to spend on clothes), I am only familiar with old time spending, when we are given carefully saved money to purchase items that are essential. This, in lower income homes, usually only happens once each year.

105
Waiting Out the Cold Winter Months in Vermont

Early this morning it was 12 below zero outside. During the months of January and February, in northern Vermont, it is bitterly cold. The ice stays all season long, making it a danger to walk and drive on. We have to be cautious on our outings.

This is the time of year when I tend to stay inside. I rarely go out, other than to church. But this Sunday morning, when I went outside to check the temperature, it was so bitterly cold, I felt numb and clumsy. I thought I'd better stay, near the hearth, at home.

There are many, in our area, who still venture out. They dress warmly and are used to this kind of weather. There are also tourists who delight in visiting for the skiing season. But for me, perhaps since I am from Massachusetts, I find it difficult to function in this biting cold. So, I stay inside.

I used to think the bitter, winter – winds, off the ocean of Massachusetts, of my childhood, were unbearable. I remember them, especially, starting in November. They were brutal. But they did not last. Not all days were windy or dreadfully freezing. When comparing those ocean winds with a common winter day in Vermont, I would say they are equal. But Winter in Vermont lasts far longer! My endurance tends to waver. I stay home a great deal.

Sometimes, I like to think of this season as a storm, when we hide under a covering, and patiently wait out the trouble. I keep indoors, while the frozen season slowly passes along. I bide my time.

I often think of the Pioneers and how they weathered many storms in winter. Perhaps they read by the fire, did their mending, baked and cooked, and did projects which cannot be done during the busy summer months. It must have been very quiet in those homes, which did not have radio, television, or computers. When it was impossible to venture out, they had church time at home with their own family as the congregation. I am sure they were always surprised and welcoming when a sudden guest appeared to visit them.

I am grateful to have company on a regular basis. My grown children are not deterred by the cold season. They go out, work, do errands, and visit me, as normal. I also love to see my grandchildren coming inside with their snowsuits, mittens, hats, and warm coats. They are rosy - cheeked and smiling!

Just a little while ago, I went out on the back grounds, of our Estate, to just walk. I know fresh air, even cold air, is essential to good health. I saw the beauty of sunlight as it touched the snowy ground. The clear blue sky, and the pretty trees, are lovely in winter. The walk was pleasant, even if it was only 7 degrees. I soon was back inside and grateful for a cozy house, a warm fire, and the luxury of hot chocolate.

I rarely spend any money in winter. The heating bills consume all we have. This is a blessing because it makes me careful. It takes away a consumer mind-set. I have to make-do, make-it-last, and do-without. This is a good discipline in frugality.

I will spend much of these winter hours waiting out the cold as I read piles of good books, do my housekeeping, and take care of my family.

The truth is, I love this time of year. It is a quiet respite from the seasons. It is a time to stop, and rest, and just enjoy being home. It is a good time to focus on prayer, and to be grateful to the Lord for all things.

106
A Christmas Break

In my childhood days, at Christmas time, school was out for the remainder of the year. We children were so happy to get to stay home for several days. We would go sledding in our large hilly yard. We would make snow-men and snow-houses. We would take walks to the corner store for treats. The snowy neighborhood would be full of children playing and families walking. Then we would go indoors to play games and read by the heater.

My mother was home with us, as most mothers were in those days. She did her usual routine of cooking, cleaning, and just puttering around the house doing projects or visiting on the telephone. She helped us with our coats, mittens, boots, and hats. She served us hot soup, and grilled cheese sandwiches, to warm us up after being out in the cold air.

We were always inventing fun things to do around the house and yard. My mother did not have to entertain us or worry about our being bored. Often, we had just received new clothes, pajamas, and some fun toys for Christmas. We were delighted to be able to spend days playing with everything.

Our house was all decorated in traditional, humble ways. There would be a Christmas song book on the piano, opened up to carols we could sing. We loved those old traditional songs! This was our favorite thing to do each afternoon. Mom would be in the kitchen, working on the laundry, or sweeping the floor, and she would suddenly hear the sound of her children, playing the piano, in the other room. I can imagine her smiling face, even now.

We had art supplies, pencils, paper, and paint. We would go from one project to another, and then do some chores, cleaning up, and then have our meals at the large kitchen table. The days always went by so quickly and then Dad would be home from work. This was the time for rest and a winding down of the day.

Our evening routine was always the same, whether we were on Christmas vacation, or enjoying a summer weekend. Dad would visit with Mother at the kitchen table and have coffee and some treat. Then mother would get our supper started, while Dad rested in the recliner. We would go from room to room talking to Mom or Dad, or just playing throughout the house, until we got that wonderful call from the kitchen saying that "supper is ready!"

On these winter nights, after we children helped clean the kitchen, Dad would start a fire in the fireplace. We would watch a television program with our parents and enjoy a quiet evening with the family.

These special times, during the Christmas season, are common in many families throughout history. This winter break, at home, is just like how it ought to be all year round. It is a happy, peaceful time. It is a time of resting from materialism and consumerism. It is a time to be with family and to have a happy home.

How wonderful it would be, if we could continue this with the coming generation of children and grandchildren - showing them, by the way we live, how precious it is to create a haven of rest for the family, in an old fashioned home.

About the Author

Mrs. White has been a housewife for more than 30 years. She is the granddaughter of a revival preacher, Mother of 5, and a Grandmother of 12.

She has been writing about homemaking on her blog, "The Legacy of Home" since 2009.

She is a retired homeschool teacher, from the Boston area. She lives with her family in an 1850's house in rural Vermont.

For more information, or to find Mrs. White's books, please visit:

The Legacy of Home Press

https://thelegacyofhomepress.blogspot.com

Also see Mrs. White's blog:

https://thelegacyofhome.blogspot.com

Made in the USA
Columbia, SC
30 March 2023

14537537R00183